Praise for *Leadership in F*

"*Leadership in Focus* is an important book and a timely one. With this new book, Vern Oakley provides an insightful, eminently readable, and highly useful approach to mastering the newest core leadership skill. Although it is clear to all that video has become one of the most important tools for leaders, it is less clear how to make the most of it to achieve mission. Oakley shows us what works and what doesn't, and in so doing, he provides us with new insights and valuable learning for all leaders."

—DANIEL WEISS, president of The Metropolitan Museum of Art

"Every business major takes a writing course, but that's not our future. Instead, everyone with something to say is going to need to say it on camera. And Vern Oakley's crash course is a great place to start."

—SETH GODIN, author of *Unleashing the Ideavirus*

"Vern Oakley is right: Video is a great tool for moving people to action. In today's 24–7 media culture, leaders need to know how to be convincing and authentic on camera. His timely approach will make effective performers out of even the most reluctant and camera shy among us."

—MARSHALL GOLDSMITH, executive coach, business educator, and *New York Times* best-selling author, ranked the number-one leadership thinker in the world by Thinkers50

"Reading *Leadership in Focus* rapidly prepares for their video shoot executives who want to make more authentic and compelling videos to connect with their organizations. The book answers questions you won't think of until after too many unsatisfactory takes. A small effort for a big ROI."

—VINCE FORLENZA, former CEO of BD

"Before you put your boss in front of the camera, put this treasure of a book in his hands."

—BLAIR ENNS, author of *The Win without Pitching Manifesto*

"Leaders know they have to be good at the podium. But in this media-intensive world, another crucial skill is looking relaxed and authoritative on camera. Vern Oakley is a seasoned director who provides a valuable service for all of us who want to project our authentic selves."

—DAVID BRANCACCIO, public radio and TV host

"In today's environment, if you don't know how to communicate authentically on camera, your brand, reputation, and impact will suffer. Vern Oakley is the perfect guide to bring film mastery to change makers, leaders, and entrepreneurs."

—PAMELA SLIM, author of *Body of Work:*
Finding the Thread that Ties Your Story Together

"Just as Vern does when he produces and directs a CEO in a corporate message video, this book guides the reader through the critical process of using the camera to create and communicate your message to the people who matter most. *Leadership in Focus* is required reading for current and future CEOs, CCOs, and all aspiring leaders!"

—PAUL BISARO, former CEO of Allergan

"This book uncovers the unstoppable power that comes from authenticity. It will be dangerous in the wrong hands . . . but a force multiplier in the right ones. After you absorb this, people who've known you as a communicator will wonder what in the hell transformed your ability to forge a connection on camera."

—DAVID C. BAKER, author of *Managing Right for the First Time*

"Modern leadership requires you to be straight, authentic, involving, and inspiring. Vern knows the maieutic art of getting all of this out of you to capture it with the eye of his camera. We used his videos as a very effective culture-building tool throughout the whole organization worldwide."

—MICHELE SCANNAVINI, former CEO of Coty

"*Leadership in Focus* is a master class in the art of effectively communicating on camera—engaging, informative, and filled with teachable moments that illustrate what to do, what to avoid, and how to become a 'suit with a soul.' Since we live in a digital video world, it should be a must-read for any leader—in a corporate setting or elsewhere—who has to communicate a vision and motivate others to take action."

—PETER LIGUORI, former CEO of Tribune Media

"No matter how experienced you are, facing a camera can be hard. Vern Oakley makes it easy. He reminds us that communication is about honesty and passion, advice that's worth following even after the shoot is over."

—MICHAEL BIERUT, partner at Pentagram Design

"As I read this book, I kept thinking nothing can impact an executive's image more than a perpetual view of their performance in a video or film. This is about the executive and the corporation. Being on film is now a for-sure in today's world. Not reading this book before you are next recorded is a mistake. Learn from decades of experience. Countless examples, tips, and considerations can prevent you from making a mistake that will live forever on a server. Not just a good read—a must read (and follow)!"

—PAUL DELFINO, author of *Avoiding Skewed Entrepreneurial Strategies*

"Vern Oakley, a master of production in the world of corporate videos and an accomplished filmmaker in his own right, uses his prodigious skills to relate to a broad audience the key elements required to communicate a message in our YouTube-driven world. Oakley furnishes a simple yet complete guide to the art of communicating authentically for the camera. *Leadership in Focus: Bringing Out Your Best on Camera* is essential reading for all who are critically concerned in conveying a message to a specific audience (something Oakley wonderfully refers to as one's "'Tribe'") with power and relevancy in our audio/visual, social media-dominated world of twenty-first century communications."

—TODD LEAVITT, former chief operating officer of NBC Studios and former president of the Television Academy

"Humans have been storytellers for tens of thousands of years, perhaps sharing news of the big hunt around the campfire. Now, video allows us to tell our stories to the world, but most executives freeze up in front of the camera. Vern shows you how to develop, deliver, and distribute your stories for maximum impact and business growth, and he does it in an engaging and approachable style. I wish I had this guide when I started creating my own videos a decade ago."

—DAVID MEERMAN SCOTT, bestselling author of
The New Rules of Marketing and PR, now in 29 languages,
from Albanian to Vietnamese.

LEADERSHIP IN
FOCUS

LEADERSHIP IN

FOCUS

BRINGING OUT
YOUR BEST
ON CAMERA

VERN OAKLEY

For CEOs, Presidents, and Aspiring Leaders

RIVER GROVE
BOOKS

Published by River Grove Books
Austin, TX
www.rivergrovebooks.com

Distributed by River Grove Books

Design and composition by Greenleaf Book Group and Kim Lance
Cover design by Greenleaf Book Group and Kim Lance
Illustrations by Taylor Lee

Publisher's Cataloging-in-Publication data is available.

Hardcover ISBN: 978-1-62634-240-8

Paperback ISBN: 978-1-966629-07-8

eBook ISBN: 978-1-62634-241-5

First Edition

To all the leaders who have shared

the sacred space between director and "actor."

Thank you for expressing your vulnerability,

your passion, and your power, and for having

the courage to trust not only me, but also yourself.

Contents

Note to Readers

The video examples referred to throughout this book, along with a host of downloadable resources to help you bring out your best on camera, can be found at vernoakley.com.

Introduction

.

It was a demanding shoot on the West Coast. I flew out to direct a video interview with a CEO. He was going on camera to announce a merger. I would take selections of his interview, and later my company would edit them together into a short but important film for the client's corporate website.

Like so many high-performing leaders, the boss was dogged by a schedule that would cripple a normal human being. His communications people swore up and down that the CEO was a totally engaging guy, at ease in any situation. He'd be great on camera. But as we started to film him, a *Twilight Zone* transformation took place. He turned into another person! He morphed into what he *thought* a CEO should look and sound like instead of just being himself.

I stopped the camera and told the crew to take a short break. I asked the boss who he imagined he was talking to while we were filming him.

"I guess I'm talking to the camera," he replied.

I continued to press him. "Who is going to watch this video?"

"Investors, employees . . . you know, stakeholders."

I then suggested another strategy. "Who do you like talking to the most about business?"

He thought for a moment. "My daughter, I guess. She's really interested in what I do. She really listens to what I'm saying."

I stepped back behind the camera and said, "OK. Let's try another take. But this time, talk to your daughter, not the camera."

He rolled his eyes a little and looked at his communications team who was sitting behind the camera. One of them lifted his eyebrows and nodded a "yes, try it."

When the camera rolled again, his answers to my questions were more relaxed. His tone and body language improved. He was being the best version of himself on camera. I could almost hear his communications people cracking smiles behind me. The CEO's delivery wasn't perfect. He made a few stumbles, but I explained that we could easily fix those in the edit. When we were wrapping to leave, I played back some footage and I could tell the guy was grudgingly pleased with his performance, especially when he said, "You ought to write a book."

As the CEO blew out of the room for his next appointment, I wondered if he'd really retained anything from our session. Would he give his next video performance much thought? Would he even care whether his next important communication to stakeholders was a video over an email or newsletter? He should, and here is why.

WHY VIDEO?

If you're reading this book, you already know video is worth considering. Perhaps it feels like the right move because video is so popular today. Or maybe your communications team is encouraging you to get on-screen and you trust their advice. But have you really stopped to think about *why* video might be the best medium for your message?

It's because, if done well, video is the communication tool that can best stir people to action.

This is not a small point. Many companies turn to video without realizing all it can accomplish. They use it to simply distribute information. Whether it's news of a merger or year-end figures, they focus on getting the words right and then have their leader read those words from a teleprompter. The video is posted, the news is shared, and the job is done. Now, there's nothing wrong with this approach, and sometimes circumstances make it necessary.

But here's the thing: You may not realize it at first, but you probably *do* want to accomplish more than just sharing news.

If the message feels important enough for video, it's likely because you want to move your audience to some kind of action. You want them to see you, connect with you, decide they stand behind your message, and then do something. If your audience is potential investors, you want them to take a stake in your company. If it's current employees, perhaps you want them to embrace new leadership or a new company initiative. If it's prospective students or employees, you want them to bring their talents to your school or organization.

In other words, you don't want your message to stop with the video. You want it to live on in your viewers so they can help you drive change. Michael Goodman, corporate communication professor at Baruch

College, defines leadership in a similar vein. He says, "A leader is some-one that you would follow to a place that you wouldn't go by yourself."[1] Your video can help you do that. It can help inspire your tribe—the people you want to influence and connect with—to do something they've never done before. And your communication leads the charge.

This purpose—the need for action—is often overlooked. It's the reason many companies don't put much thought or time into preparing for an effective video performance. They don't realize how much video can do for them if the leader on-screen makes an emotional connection with his or her audience. It can go as far as building a culture and creating your legacy as a leader, as others engage with your vision.

Before I go on, let me clarify that this book talks specifically about the professionally produced, short videos that are typically shared on a company's intranet, or publicly via an organization's website and/or video platforms like YouTube. I talk about these videos within the context of film because, in my business, the word film has come to mean motion pictures of all kinds—from feature-length animation to online videos. A company video may be a far cry from a feature-length movie, but each format is powered by the same fundamental principles of film.

Film is beloved in cultures worldwide in large part because it's such a powerful vehicle for storytelling. Stories connect humans in a way that not much else can. We turn to them to understand ourselves, and others, and as we share our stories with one another, we slowly build a legacy, a culture, a country, or even a company. It's no wonder our society has become obsessed with video. With the tap of a screen and two minutes of our time, we're able to see, hear, and make a personal connection with someone's story in a way that's second only to being with them live.

CONNECTION = ACTION

I talk a lot about authentic leadership throughout this book because it's the key ingredient for effective videos. The point is to be comfortable in your own skin, show your people who you truly are, that you care about them, and that you're working together toward a greater goal. Communicating with authenticity is no longer optional in the digital age. Gone are the days when a company's main concern was to keep shareholders happy. Today *all* stakeholders want to know what you're up to—from employees to customers and everyone in between.

It's often said that millennials demand transparency and authenticity from businesses, but let's face it: We all want that transparency today. I'm grateful to millennials for bringing attention to such a critical point. Business leaders need to step up and communicate honestly and openly if they want to inspire action. It's the only chance they have to make an emotional connection with their audience.

That emotional connection is the big difference between videos that simply share information and those that evoke action. To be sure, you'll have a captive audience if viewers are personally invested in your video's topic. It doesn't matter how you deliver the message—if you're announcing something like bonuses or layoffs, viewers will hang on every word. But if you want them to do more than listen—if you want them to act—your audience needs to feel a connection with you.

Humans are social creatures. We need to connect with others and feel that we're part of a tribe. We make sense of life and the world around us through the connections we make and the stories we tell. Since the beginning of civilization, every tribe has had a storyteller. If you're the leader of an organization, that storyteller is going to be you.

Even if you have a trusted team to help you craft your messages, more often than not, you will be the one to deliver them to your people.

Don't worry if you don't see yourself as a storyteller, or if you've only ever used video to share information. The fact is, information leads to understanding, and getting your audience to understand your message is incredibly important. But understanding alone does not trigger action. Emotions lead people to action. This is where storytelling can help you take your videos to the next level, and you don't need to fancy yourself a novelist to tap into this effective tool. Your stories can be as simple as brief memories that show your audience you're a living, breathing human.

Let's go back to the heart of communication basics. To craft an effective message, you have to ask, "Who is my audience? What do I want that audience to think, do, feel, say, buy, or buy into when they hear my message?" This may seem like nothing more than a subtle shift in the way you think of video, but the difference is profound. Through this new lens, making a video is no longer about the information you want to convey. It's about the audience you want to reach.

When you walk onto a film set it's easy to forget you're making a video to connect with a large audience. I've seen many leaders approach filming as if they've come to answer my interview questions, forgetting the broader audience they hope to reach. David Brancaccio, host of American Public Media's *Marketplace Morning Report*, often witnesses this mistake when guests appear on his show. "They prepare for the conversation as if they're only there to talk to me, one-on-one. They treat the session like a casual talk and forget that I'm actually just the collection point through which they'll be speaking to hundreds of thousands of people."[2]

Now, it's fine to imagine speaking to one specific person as a way of putting yourself at ease. The CEO I mentioned previously did this when he pretended to be talking to his daughter. Just don't forget that you're communicating on a much larger scale. Ideally, you'd take the time to think about how you want your message to resonate with that larger crowd, and prepare your appearance with that goal in mind. What if you could speak to each and every audience member with the same level of connection and intimacy as the CEO did speaking to his daughter?

A leader who connects with his or her audience—whether on-screen or off—has the potential to drive real progress. Anyone can have a high-ranking title, but as John Maxwell said in *The 21 Irrefutable Laws of Leadership*, "True leadership cannot be . . . assigned. It comes only from influence. . . . It must be earned."[3] A first step in earning influence is to let your people know who you are—that you're trustworthy, that you care about them and your shared work, and that you have what it takes to lead them to success. Your people simply won't follow you if they don't believe in you.

AN AGENT FOR CHANGE

Your video communications can help you earn influence, but to bond with your audience you need to take off the mask that many of us in leadership positions tend to wear. You have to let viewers see the vulnerable, human person behind your message. This is the game changer when it comes to making an effective video. It doesn't matter whether you're a millennial who is used to having the iPhone camera pointed at you or a baby boomer who feels uncomfortable in front of the lens.

The big goal is to reveal who you really are. Now, to be clear, you need to follow up your video communications with great work every day, but you'll be working in vain if your tribe doesn't know you or your vision.

> "It is the capacity to develop and improve their skills that distinguishes leaders from followers."
>
> **—WARREN BENNIS**

Your first step in connecting with viewers is to show them you care. At the most basic level, this means that any video you participate in should strive for high-quality content and the appropriate production value. You and/or your advisors should be as involved as possible in maximizing your video's strategy, content, and style. The end result will show your viewer that you care enough about them to deliver your best. The return on investment will be a stronger connection to those you want to reach; heightened respect, prestige, and interest in your organization; a stronger brand; and a much better legacy.

Leadership in Focus is written for leaders who realize that it's not just what you say on camera that's important—it's how you say it. It doesn't matter whether you're a CEO, a middle manager, or a budding entrepreneur making YouTube videos to influence your tribe. The principles in this book will help anyone who wants to rally others around a message.

The lessons here are equally applicable to the communications professionals who support these leaders. As a part of a leader's trusted team, they are on the front lines when the camera rolls. They likely have the greatest influence on a leader's on-camera appearance, and the advice here will help them *help you*.

In the chapters ahead I'll walk you through the steps you should take to prepare for a powerful on-camera appearance. You can read from cover to cover, or jump to a chapter that you're particularly interested in.

You may be familiar with some of the concepts we'll cover here, but it's worth unpacking them in this new context so you can see how they fit within the bigger picture. Because while the goal is to *just be yourself* on camera, it takes a good amount of practice and preparation to accomplish being yourself when the camera is rolling. This may be why so many high-performing leaders are disappointed by how they come across on camera. Even if you don't freeze up in front of the lens, a great video performance requires you to approach your communications in a new way.

Becoming effective on camera requires a specific skill set. A crucial step toward that goal is learning to channel your real, emotional self. I'll spend an entire chapter looking at authenticity and the pistons that drive it: courage and vulnerability. I'll show you how leaders managed to connect with their audience through well-prepared on-camera appearances that had a proven and positive impact on their influence—and as a result, on their organization's success, morale, and bottom line. We'll also see how badly conceived and poorly executed presentations can have the opposite effect—low morale, distrust, and a lack of camaraderie throughout an organization. Most importantly, I will show you how to be your true self on camera—a critical skill all great leaders must master, and one that will help you well beyond your video appearances.

We'll explore the role of the professional film crew and the total effort needed to make your on-camera appearance resonate. The sole job of your director, cameraman, sound, lighting, and makeup pros is to make you look and sound great. We'll also look at how some of history's most brazen leaders influenced the way we connect with one another today.

Why listen to me? Because for over three decades I've directed thousands of people, from famous performing artists to *Fortune* 500 CEOs to factory workers to college presidents, on the art of communicating authentically on camera. Through coaching and conversation, I've helped them present their ideas and visions on video without appearing overbearing or stiff. I've worked with them to hone the content of *what* they want to say and showed them *how to say* it from one human being to another. My insights are also paired with wisdom from PR professionals and corporate communication advisors—as well as the leaders who have learned from these masters of communication.

I wrote *Leadership in Focus* because I think authentic video communications can start the kinds of dialogues we need to reboot and repurpose our society for the better. I want to share what I've learned to help you boost your influence by becoming your best self on camera. Who knows? As you lead your people to action, you might just change the world.

And—action!

PART I

THE VIDEO MIND-SET

1

Never a Better Time
to Be on Camera

"No art passes our conscience in the way film
does, and goes directly to our feelings."

—INGMAR BERGMAN

It's hard to imagine that film has only been around for a little over a century. When compared to artistic media like music, painting, and sculpture, film is practically in its infancy. And that's true of film in general. This book zeroes in on something much newer than that—the idea of leaders appearing on-screen to connect with their audience. Scientists are just starting to measure the effects of how individuals express themselves on camera. It's an exciting time. The brave people who already embrace video have been doing so without much knowledge as to how their appearances influence viewers. They know they can leverage their in-person communication skills in front of the lens, but a lot more goes into great video performances than most people realize.

The first leader to truly leverage film's benefits was John F. Kennedy when he went up against Richard Nixon in the 1960 presidential debates. As he prepared for the debates, Kennedy had to have sensed the potential of television when he asked American film director Arthur Penn (*Bonnie and Clyde, The Miracle Worker*, etc.) to coach him on how to behave on camera. Penn helped him learn to relax and urged Kennedy to be himself—down to that "Hahvud Yahd" Boston accent.

The debates were broadcast on television and radio. Radio listeners thought Nixon outperformed Kennedy, yet TV watchers came to the opposite conclusion. Nixon was nervous and sweaty; Kennedy was personable and confident. The election was close, but JFK won and, as *TIME* magazine noted, many attributed his edge to his brilliant on-camera performance.[1]

The Kennedy–Nixon debates proved that a powerful on-camera appearance could eclipse the impact of the spoken word. Since then, politicians have turned television appearances into something akin to an art form. From Ronald Reagan to Al Franken to Donald Trump, politicians' on-camera skills have greatly enhanced their political impact. Business leaders followed politicians' lead as some of industry's biggest icons began to appear on camera. In the 1980s, Chrysler hired famed documentary filmmakers Albert and David Maysles to direct a series of videos that were shown to Chrysler dealers.[2] They were among the first videos in which CEO Lee Iacocca appeared, and they marked the beginning of a video journey that eventually led to Iacocca starring in several television commercials that resurrected the company's image.

The Maysles brought their famed direct cinema style to Chrysler's in-house videos. True to their method, the brothers didn't set up false scenarios or glorify reality. They strictly adhered to capturing Iacocca's true personality, which was refreshing given the artificiality of films and documentaries at the time. A 1982 *New York Times* article about the Maysles' corporate work noted that "the number of four-letter words enunciated by the Chrysler chairman [in those videos] seems to exceed the number of Chryslers sold last year."

In that same article, the brothers were quick to tell the *Times* that they did not have an affinity toward most corporate videos. David was quoted saying, "Most of these sales films [are] not very good. They're dull, they're done by committee, they're stiff." Albert shared his brother's disdain, "Most corporate films start as a puff piece, continue as a puff piece, and end as a puff piece. So no one's interested."[3]

Unfortunately, not much has changed in three decades. Now more than ever, viewers crave the raw honesty that the Maysles brought to life in their films. Even though we may never meet our political leaders, we expect to get to know them through their on-camera appearances. Millennials, in particular, see straight through the veneer when a leader tries to be someone they're not, whether on camera or off. But many organizations still opt for puff pieces over truth-telling, and viewers are forced to fill in the blanks about whatever they think their leaders might not be telling them.

Working with the Maysles on Chrysler's in-house videos helped Iacocca show his true self to viewers. By the time he was ready for national TV commercials, his booming personality nearly jumped through the screen and into viewers' living rooms.

Ad executive Leo-Arthur Kelmenson got the idea to have Iacocca star in a series of Chrysler commercials to help pull the company out of its slump. Iacocca's mission was to assure America that "The pride is back" (the name of their ad campaign) and that the government's

1979 bailout was taxpayer money well spent. Few leaders had appeared on camera like this before. At stake were the CEO's reputation and the jobs of thousands of employees.

The commercials featured Iacocca strutting across the factory floor spouting straight talk about Chrysler's quality and innovation. It was Iacocca essentially being himself. He looked straight into the camera and challenged Americans with from-the-heart lines like "If you can find a better car, buy it." The ads made Iacocca an icon for the American comeback and helped pull Chrysler out of its financial death spiral.[4]

Now, we're not Lee Iacocca or JFK. But the good news is, these days we don't have to be. You don't need to buy an expensive TV commercial spot (although you can) or wait for your chance to be in a nationally televised debate to engage with a wide audience through film. All you need is a well-made video, an Internet connection, and great on-camera communication. These last details can't be underestimated.

WE LIVE IN A DIGITAL VIDEO WORLD

According to Cisco, 82 percent of all Internet traffic will be video by 2020.[5] Learning to communicate effectively on camera is not a choice for leaders anymore; it's a necessity because we live in a digital *video* world. Gone are the days when authentic video appearances like Iacocca's were a novelty. Video is now ubiquitous, and it's changed the way we're expected to do business. Today's audiences want to see leaders talking to them through computers, phones, and tablets at the drop of a hat. According to a study coauthored by *Forbes* and Google, three-quarters of executives surveyed said they watch work-related videos on business websites at least weekly, and half surveyed were apt to share videos with colleagues.[6]

Technology moves so quickly that modern video platforms are in their infancy. Social media, YouTube, and business-focused video outlets like Kickstarter evolve every day, and there's no telling how new apps are going to affect the way video is distributed and consumed in the future. Tech is also constantly changing the recording mechanisms, the playback mechanisms, and how we work with the material. In 2015, the first feature film shot entirely on an iPhone was released at the Sundance Film Festival. At the time of this writing, iPhones already shoot at a higher resolution than HD. Technology informs how we view and create films, but it doesn't change the vital need to understand communication, body language, storytelling, and honesty. Those elements are timeless.

Whether you lead a *Fortune* 500 company, a university, a start-up, or a nonprofit—your on-camera appearances will affect your organization's future. Global culture has embraced video as the ultimate communications currency, but so far, many leaders are failing their audiences. According to a survey, 74 percent of consumers feel that open, transparent communication is critical to effective leadership, but only 29 percent feel their leaders communicate effectively.[7] People naturally see their leader as an icon of the organization they run. If you want to connect with the people, you have to go where they are. You have to reach them through their screen.

Shrinking attention spans also mean your video has to be short and captivating. In no more than a few minutes, you need to hook readers with a story, communicate your message, and incite action. Once it's posted online, your video is likely to live on the Internet, or on your company's intranet, twenty-four hours a day, indefinitely. Every time viewers watch it, they will experience your message exactly the way you intended it to reach them.

It doesn't matter where we are these days. The Internet and smart phones let us connect with our audience anywhere, at any time. This makes video the next best thing to delivering important news to employees, customers, or other stakeholders around the world in person—especially in cases when an email or memo absolutely will not do. It lets us control our message and show people who we really are during times when they need to know we're there for them.

We have the power to connect with audiences that are infinitely larger than those that Iacocca and JFK spent their lifetimes (and major corporate dollars) trying to reach. But our viewers can easily dismiss us if we seem untrustworthy. If you turn into a sweaty Nixon when the tape begins to roll, viewers won't hang on long enough to even hear your story. Or worse, they'll watch, but they won't believe a word you're saying.

Forget the slick performances that showcase the leader you *think* you should be. Those charades fool no one, and they push you further away from the people you want to connect with the most. The best leaders know how to let down their guard and communicate their vision, human-to-human, with every person they hope to reach.

VIDEO'S SECRET SAUCE

Video is wildly different from a recorded speech, where the camera never cuts away from the subject, or a live performance, where the audience and speaker can share an energy or rhythm by being in the same room. Video is distinct in that its creators leverage the practices of film in order to craft a brief, powerful final piece. A professional video team can edit hours of interview footage into a few short minutes containing only your essential ideas. Other tools like B-roll—alternate footage interwoven with your speaking parts—can help viewers see a human side of your message that goes beyond the words or even your non-verbals. B-roll can be anything from shots of you playing with your dog to an exciting interaction with colleagues. I'll talk about these topics in more detail throughout the book.

It will only get easier to create effective videos as technology and film methods advance. On the extreme end, Japan is already using robot newscasters that appear strikingly real. Now, we're probably a long way from being able to replace you with your robotic twin, but the advice in this book should help you relax enough so you won't feel you need one.

TIMELESS WISDOM FOR A MODERN AGE

As innovations soar, our longtime mentors often still possess the timeliest wisdom. I studied with JFK's TV coach Arthur Penn for years and I deeply admire his work. I hadn't realized Penn had possibly changed the course of US history until I read his *New York Times* obituary. The article notes, "Mr. Penn's instructions to Kennedy—to look directly into the camera and keep his responses brief and pithy—helped give Kennedy an aura of confidence and calm that created a vivid contrast to Nixon, his more experienced but less telegenic Republican rival."[8]

This point helped me see that I'd been applying the concepts I'd learned from Penn and other teachers about acting, performance, and authenticity in theater and film to every person I've directed on camera. Penn inadvertently taught me that in a world laden with wooden video appearances, the best way to stand out is to show that you're a real, accessible human. His wisdom is still relevant decades later, and even more today, as we're glued to our devices and constantly craving human connection. The need for human connection is primal. It's a big reason I decided to write this book.

Never a Better Time to Be on Camera—Key Ideas

▶ Film is a fairly young art form. Not much study has gone into how individuals express themselves on camera.

▶ The first leaders to leverage film were politicians, but business leaders soon followed suit. Video is experiencing a renaissance as more and more leaders turn to video to connect with their tribe.

▶ Honest video communication is no longer a novelty. Audiences expect their leaders to communicate with them on-screen, and shrinking attention spans mean we have to make an emotional connection almost instantly.

▶ Producers can leverage film practices to craft a brief but powerful final piece.

I hope the chapters ahead will move you to make the most of your video appearances, because there's never been a better time to be on camera. Every appearance is a chance to build your culture, communicate your vision, and engage and inspire others. Your tribe is waiting for you to get real on their screen. Are you ready to show them who their leader truly is?

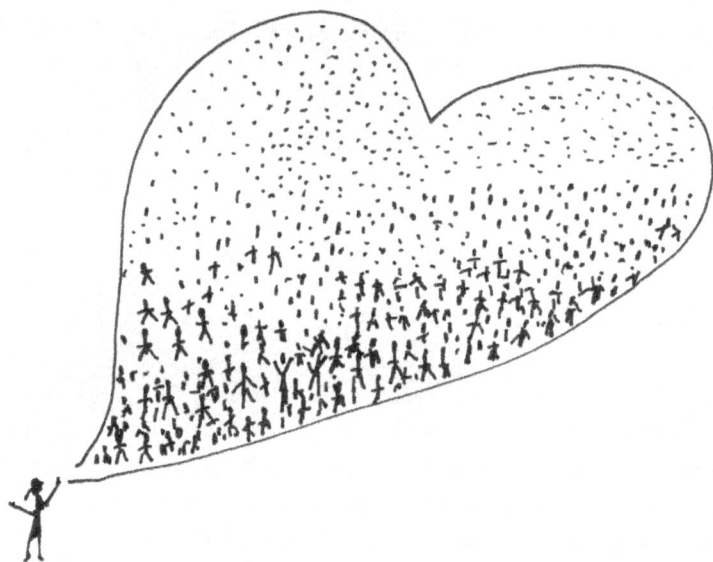

2

Speak from Your Heart: Connect with Millions

"The cave you fear to enter holds the treasure you seek."

—JOSEPH CAMPBELL

My assignment was to direct the CEO of an international company in the entertainment industry. The leader was an urbane, continental woman who was sophisticated in matters of the media. She was, understandably, very busy, so busy she didn't have any prep time available to speak to me before the shoot.

The film would be shown on her company's private intranet. She had just been appointed CEO after her predecessor, who was beloved by the company, had stepped down. Tens of thousands of people would see her share her vision for the first time. She would be speaking directly to all of her employees, hoping to inspire them, connect with them, and make sure they were all working toward her new vision for the company. A lot was riding on this shoot.

The CEO knew her information well enough to discuss it on camera without a teleprompter. (See chapter 10 for more about the teleprompter.) When we finally met, I suggested she speak directly to the camera when she answered my interview questions. The kind of communication she was delivering is most intimate and powerful done this way. She immediately said, "I don't want to do that." Given her lack of preparation, who could blame her? It's hard to look directly into the camera. It feels cold and uncomfortable, but the end result is anything but.

OK, so maybe she wouldn't look into the camera, but I needed to help this CEO realize that this one short shoot, this brief interlude in her day, offered her the rare opportunity to demonstrate courage, imagination, emotion, and brio to tens of thousands of employees at once. It's crucial for anyone about to go on camera to have this mind-set.

My job was not to do the shoot the way I wanted; my job was to help this leader engage. Since I preach the virtues of authenticity, I had to step out on a limb and do something authentic. As firmly and diplomatically as I could, I said, "We'll do whatever you want if you help me help you to find a way to speak from your heart." This got her attention.

I explained that a more humanizing presentation would hold the viewers' attention and help them connect with her ideas. I suggested we shoot her in action interacting with her staff, and out on the street walking around her neighborhood. I begged her to be spontaneous and to answer off-the-cuff questions to which she had no prepared answers. She thought this over for several long seconds, shook her head, and said curtly, "I don't want to do that."

Her answer was the classic response to an unfamiliar situation where a person feels vulnerable, something I've seen often throughout my career. Many shoots begin with some kind of negative, dismissive power remark. For example, one executive said, "Let's just get this over with!" I don't blame leaders for being careful, but I also don't have to take a negative as a "no."

As we talked, I learned the CEO didn't lack courage, imagination, or humanity. The real problem was simple. Because of her jam-packed schedule, she wasn't prepared. I explained that the communications team and I had tried to get on her schedule to prep her. She knew this was true. So I said we could prep her then, we could make it work in the time allotted. And I reminded her if she were ever unhappy with a take, we would simply do another one and only link the best performances together in our edits.

I think the CEO sensed the seriousness of my frustration and decided my convictions were worth her time. She was willing to try something new. Once she made the decision, she threw herself at the challenge. My crew and I filmed her speaking directly to the camera about her love for the company. We used three camera angles, which let us condense her one-hour interview into a short, coherent piece. We balanced the interview with footage of her having genuine interactions with colleagues around the office. This kind of B-roll was the perfect way to show the new leader in time and space. We simply put her together with people with whom she had business to talk about, and let the camera roll. Viewers could see her real excitement as she exchanged ideas with colleagues and her whole team's genuine warmth and camaraderie toward one another. We also sprinkled in shots of her riding the subway to work with colleagues who lived in her neighborhood.

The resulting film was a revelation. By being herself, the leader came through like gangbusters; her native charm, intelligence, and devotion to her company were indisputable in her statements. Nothing she did was made up. She really did ride the subway to work with colleagues and she really did love her job. The film made a lasting and positive impression with stakeholders because it celebrated her human spirit. She was not only great on camera, she was authentically great—because she spoke from her heart.

Her video was also a great example of the wonders of editing. I'll talk more about this in later chapters, but as you ease into the idea of video, remember that the pressure isn't all on you to make a fantastic film. That's why you have a production crew. They will blend your presentation with B-roll, music, and tactful editing to create a powerful viewing experience that you will be proud of.

BECOMING A SUIT WITH SOUL

When people hear titles like CEO or president, the words conjure up some remote "suit" sitting in a corner suite on the top floor, a king or queen with feet of clay they will never meet. Video is one of the best ways to convey to the majority of employees that there's a real beating heart under the Brooks Brothers blazer. Video can reach any number of people, anywhere, at any time, while allowing the speaker to show his or her humanity. Our subway-riding CEO showed her human side by letting us balance candid footage with a direct, passionate address to employees about her goals for the company. By the end of the video, the only stereotypical thing about this "suit" was, well, her suit. But nobody was paying attention to her clothes by that point.

Sometimes when I sense that a leader I'm filming is uncomfortable, I discover that he or she has a preconceived notion of how a leader should look and act. And I sense deep down these leaders are trying to fake it. As they talk on camera, you can almost hear their true selves saying, "I never talk like this. This is nonsense. What am I saying? Why am I acting like this?" This is when it's important to ease their fears and speak truth to power. I don't want them to mimic some hypercontrolled posture they *think* a leader should assume—and neither does anybody else.

When leaders unpack their content on camera, their message is simply the freight on the train. In order for the freight or content to resonate en masse, the public must know that the conductor is for real. Is this someone they'd trust to transport their enterprise through adversity and into the future? Does he or she care about people or only about profits? Does a heart beat beneath the suit? Forget trying to live up to your image of what a leader should look like. All you need to do is just focus on looking like *you*.

I've made it my business to help leaders speak from the heart by helping them overcome their fear of exposing their humanity and vulnerability on camera. I've taught leaders that those who do their homework and speak to others as fellow humans have more credibility. Some of them have even told me they've become better leaders in the process.

Exposing vulnerabilities to establish your humanity requires introspection and risk taking. There's no evolutionary imperative for us as a species to perform on camera. To make the task of doing so even more challenging, leaders today need to project themselves to an increasingly complex world and an increasingly complex set of environments. It's not only on a face-to-face basis, but it's multichannel, cross-border, and cross-cultural. I've come to see that few leaders have the time (or frankly the interest) to explore the psychological elements of what it takes to be genuine on camera, especially when there's pressure to connect on so many levels. It's a daunting prospect. If this describes you, don't worry. Nobody expects you to go from zero to authentic overnight, but this book offers strategies that can help you unlock your true self in front of the lens sooner than you may think was possible.

It's especially critical to cut through the noise if you lead a large organization. Connecting with your tribe is the only way to make your vision crystal clear to everyone. You want them to know exactly what everyone in the organization is working to achieve. Jim Tusty, a longtime producer who has filmed leaders at Coca-Cola, GE, and Raytheon, among many other places, has seen this important issue play out among his clients. He points out that oftentimes, companies seem to think that if a CEO explains his vision clearly to his top-level leaders, those leaders will communicate the exact same message to those below them.

"The false assumption is that the SVP is going to talk to the VP, who's going to talk to the managers, who's going to talk to the next level, until you get those frontline people," says Tusty. He goes on to explain that two things happen in this scenario. The first is unintentional miscommunication. It's a game of telephone with lots of opportunity for things to get misunderstood. The other is the inevitable midlevel manager who disagrees with the CEO and is saying to himself or herself, "I don't agree with that. That's not how this company has done it. We've always turned right. That's what I'm going to do." The midlevel manager is in open disagreement because it's difficult to see the big picture from his perspective, and the CEO's vision may contradict the manager's personal interests. "Direct communication from the CEO is critical," Tusty says. "Then every employee in the organization will understand the top-line message, the main direction, and no middle manager can mess that up."[1]

The benefits of communicating directly with everyone on the ladder go beyond just the words you speak. Studies in neuroscience prove that a leader's emotions, mood, and tone deeply affect those who look to them for guidance. An article in Six Seconds highlights emotional intelligence icon Daniel Goleman's explanation of "mirror neurons," which are "a kind of 'neural wi-fi' that monitors what is happening in other people." He says, "This system tracks their emotions, what movements they're making, what they intend, and it activates, in our brains, precisely the same brain areas as are active in the other person. This puts us on the same wavelength and it does it automatically, instantaneously, and unconsciously."[2]

When applying this concept to business, Goleman goes on to explain that the leader's internal state affects employees' mind-sets and their ability to perform. Interestingly, mirror neurons don't discriminate between in-person interactions and those on-screen. In fact, studies by one of the discoverers of mirror neurons, neuroscientist Vittorio Gallese, confirm that when we see someone do or feel something on film, the same areas that would be active in that person's brain are also activated in our own. It doesn't matter whether the other person is on-screen or in the room with us.[3]

So effective video communication won't only clarify your message. Your on-screen vibe can literally contribute to shaping the culture you want your company to have.

WRITING YOUR OWN STORY

The term authenticity is often bandied about in business books and media. For some, it has come to signify a kind of permanent state, once attained. But authenticity is anything but. It is a philosophical and existential state that, for me, means you're constantly working on being true to yourself and to your beliefs. The word is often used to describe one quality of a great leader. People want to follow leaders who are real. They want to be led by people who work hard to find and refine their true selves.

A simple way to look at authenticity is to see it as writing your own story. Each time you appear on video you're unveiling a new chapter. So, whose story do you want to write? Is it the story of a leader who is true to herself and her beliefs, and who stands by her people? Someone who works hard to grow and encourages her people to grow with her? Or do you prefer to recite lines from a role to which you've been assigned by the status quo, by society, or your own imagined rulebook? Audiences crave authenticity partly as a reaction to political and economic turbulence. The public has become disenchanted with business people and politicians who seem to only say what they think people want to hear. We don't want slick leaders anymore. We demand sincerity, honesty, and integrity. We want our leaders to be real human beings.

When Tony Cicatiello, head of CN Communications, managed the political campaigns of future New Jersey governor Tom Kean, two words summed up his advice to the candidate: *Be yourself.* Tony recalls, "When we were hiring consultants to join the Kean campaign, one of them said, 'Well your name is spelled Kean, you pronounce it Cane. You should change it to "keen," and you talk funny, you have this gap in your teeth, you probably should have your teeth fixed.' So we fired that person. We all have flaws. But everybody likes people who have flaws. We all realize that we're human."[4]

If Kean had hired that consultant and taken his advice, he would have spent the campaign telling someone else's story—someone who doesn't even exist. Nobody would have believed in him because Kean wouldn't have even believed himself.

The first step to being authentic on camera is to be yourself. But remember that striving for authenticity is a lifelong process. It's something you need to work on continuously because your story evolves as you grow each day.

To start, look back at your roots and the people and events that helped shape you. Take a risk by asking those friends, colleagues, and relatives what they think your strengths and weaknesses are. Ask for their honest feedback and listen carefully. Their observations may be way off from how you see yourself, but this is a good thing. They're illuminating your blind spots to help you see the real you. Work to be open, to listen, and to think about how you might leverage your strengths on video, and perhaps those newly discovered weaknesses too. If you're willing to truly hear and act on trusted feedback, you'll quickly discover that the actions you take will permeate and benefit much of your work as a leader—not just your video appearance.

Another great way to get a handle on this elusive term is to look at leaders who have exhibited the signature traits that lead to authenticity: showing vulnerability and courage. Such is the story of a reluctant king who inspired the free world. His extraordinary story speaks volumes about the magic that occurs when effective communication is coupled with authentic leadership.

> "Knowing yourself is the beginning of all wisdom."
>
> —ARISTOTLE

A KING AHEAD OF HIS TIME

In 1939 a nervous forty-four-year-old monarch sat behind a microphone. Millions of people were waiting at their radios to hear what he had to say. The subject was the survival of civilization. The man was George VI, the king of the British Empire.

Nicknamed "Bertie" by the royal family, he ran the gauntlet of childhood disabilities from being knock-kneed to having uncontrollable stammering. Painful splints straightened the bone deformities, but the stammering dogged him into adulthood. The middle-aged monarch was about to prepare his subjects across the globe to go to war against Nazi Germany.

Bertie never wanted to be king. The title was thrust on him when his brother abdicated. But now that he wore the crown, George VI was determined to become an effective leader. His goal was to use mass communication to inspire courage, hope, and the commitment to a fight for freedom. Stumbling on his words would have the opposite effect.

Long before the speech, the king began working intensively with a voice therapist in London. And in the days before the radio address, the monarch took an active role in shaping what he was about to say. As he faced the microphone, he was certain his message was true. The question was whether he could deliver it clearly. He knew that in this moment, his people needed to see him as the courageous and confident leader that he was. There was no time for stammering and fumbling his words, as everyone knew he did. On that day, they needed to see him as a leader who could carry them through a terrible situation that they weren't able to face on their own.

As the king began to speak, there were long pauses and a few minor mumbles, but his confidence grew with each word. His opening sentence was simple and from the heart. Instead of speaking to the masses, he spoke to each listener individually.

> In this grave hour, perhaps the most fateful in our history, I send to every household of my peoples, both at home and overseas, this message, spoken with the same depth of feeling for each one of you as if I were able to cross your threshold and speak to you myself.[5]

Now, I want to be clear that giving a speech, especially on radio, is very different from appearing on video, but there's still so much to learn from Bertie's iconic broadcast. To start, the world thought

Bertie was nearly incapable of speaking publicly, so by the time he successfully uttered the last words of his message, the king's courage turned his subjects into followers. His actions told the story of a leader whose people now saw as someone they could trust. Everyone knew how hard he had worked to simply be able to speak through that microphone to reach them. It was a major stride in earning influence with his people. By exposing his own humanity and vulnerability, George VI rallied his empire and proved he was a true and authentic leader.

George VI's speech is also one of history's first examples of what can happen when a leader leverages the power of mass media to connect with his or her people. Bertie didn't just stand at a podium and give a speech. He went to the place where his audience liked to hear stories. In 1939, that place was radio. In 1960, JFK knew it was critical to connect with people through their television sets. And today, we need to meet our audience where they're looking the most: online videos. Bertie figured out, decades before others, that the best way to rally your tribe is to share your story wherever your people go to listen.

> **"The highest of distinctions is service to others."**
>
> **—KING GEORGE VI**

KNOWING WHICH SIDE TO SHOW

Bertie's famed broadcast reveals another great lesson in authenticity: It's important to know which side of yourself to show in a given situation. We all have different sides to our authentic selves that we can manage and project depending on the specific communication goals. To be authentic doesn't mean telling people everything about yourself or ticking off a list of vulnerabilities. You can share, instead, the one side of yourself that is most appropriate for the specific video. In Bertie's case, he knew his call to war didn't have room for stuttering. So he worked to address the issue to allow his other qualities—confidence and courage—to shine.

Jean Tomlin, former HR director at Marks and Spencer, is quoted in a *Harvard Business Review* article on this very topic. She says she considers the needs and expectations of the people she's communicating with when she decides which part of her personality to share.

"I want to be me, but I am channeling parts of me to the context," she said. "What you get is a segment of me. It is not a fabrication or a façade—just the bits that are relevant for that situation."[6]

The article's authors posit that "great leaders seem to know which personality traits they should reveal to whom and when. They are capable of adapting to the demands of the situations they face and the people they lead, yet they do not lose their identities in the process. Authentic leaders remain focused on where they are going but never lose sight of where they came from." This idea especially resonates when it comes to your video appearances. A merger that involves potential risk might require a more circumspect but optimistic *you* on camera. A video highlighting your company's next innovation offers room for you to geek out talking about the work that allowed you and your team to get this far. You are *yourself* in every context, but you're choosing the right version of *you* for each place and time.

Sometimes authenticity can shine through with just a few powerful words. During the 2008 presidential campaign, Senator John McCain defended his opponent at a televised town meeting. When some in the crowd shouted out that Barack Obama was a "liar" and a "terrorist," McCain said, "We want to fight, and I will fight, but I will be respectful. I admire Senator Obama and his accomplishments, and I will respect him."[7] He stared straight at the hecklers; his posture was natural but resolute. After the senator from Arizona said what he had to say, everyone could see that he meant it, even those in the crowd who booed him. This was a true leader speaking from the heart in a few brief words. It didn't take a long, drawn-out speech for McCain to show viewers his humanity in that moment. In fact, this act of courage may have revealed more about McCain as a leader than anything he could have said during an hours-long presidential debate.

Another way to share one of your human sides—perhaps more intentionally than McCain did in the previous example—is to talk about what you love. As a director, I make a point of asking leaders about their passions and then I find a way to sprinkle these little details into their video performances. When you talk about your passions on camera, your authenticity will shine through and your audience will feel they've gotten to know you. They'll want to listen to what you have to say afterward. You're headed up the mountain and you want to make sure your people are following you.

I said previously that you don't need to see yourself as a storyteller to work in personal details. I mean it—just a couple of extra words can have a big impact. For example, say you're opening a new plant in South Carolina. You could say something as simple as, "I've always loved South Carolina because my family and I used to vacation here when I was a boy." If you're talking about competition in your industry, you could say something like, "It's tough competing in this space, but I have to say I'm a very competitive guy. I won the chili cook-off in my town three years in a row."

It's these small personal touch points that humanize us. You can mention them quickly, without ever getting off topic. But your love for your shared work also has to shine through with vigor if people are going to see you as a leader worth following. As we will discover in a later chapter, being prepared and knowing your material intimately is another key to a successful video appearance, and it's essential in building trust among your viewers. Knowing the facts, figures, and other details of your message shows that you're invested in your work and that you're capable of guiding your people.

SpaceX founder Elon Musk shows such genuine excitement for his work in a video interview with actor Joseph Gordon-Levitt,[8] that his enthusiasm would outshine that of a toddler at Disney World. Yet he's fully composed and professional throughout the interview. The video captures Musk talking about his plans to revolutionize space travel and establish Mars as a self-sustaining civilization. He opens by saying, "If you asked anyone what were some of the greatest things that happened in the 20th century, I think they'd say, 'We landed on the moon.' That's freakin' awesome!"[9] His passion for space travel nearly reverberates off the screen and is instantly contagious.

When asked what would need to happen for people to live on Mars, Musk dishes the science in a way that's easy to understand and funny. He refers to Mars as a "fixer-upper of a planet" and explains the practical steps needed to make its atmosphere habitable for humans. It's hard to imagine that any talk of "releasing greenhouse gasses" could be exciting, but Musk's fervor for his work has viewers hanging on every detail.

The video also shows us how painless and relatable storytelling can be, again, even if you don't see yourself as a natural storyteller. In just a few seconds, Musk tells the interviewer that *Star Wars* had a big impact on him because it was the first movie he'd ever seen. He even named SpaceX's Falcon rocket after the *Millennium Falcon*, the iconic spacecraft in *Star Wars*. This brief anecdote lets us see Musk as the daydreaming child that so many viewers can relate to. It took literally seconds for him to make that connection with viewers.

Ultimately, the opportunities to show your authenticity are limitless. The real *you* may shine in a brief moment of expressing your values, as we saw with John McCain, or you can take a bit more time to plan what you'll say. That's one of the great benefits of video—you are in a safe space. You can work with your communications team and director trying several approaches until you feel totally comfortable. This isn't a media interview where someone might try to put you on the spot or catch you off guard. And even if your final performance is not flawless, your viewers won't mind. They just want to know that they're hearing from a honest-to-goodness human.

Speak from Your Heart: Connect with Millions—Key Ideas

▶ Forget what you think a leader should look like on camera. Your video will have more influence if you show the real, human you.

▶ It's especially important to communicate directly with your audience if you lead a large organization. If you rely on others to share your message, it's all too easy for it to be misinterpreted by the time it reaches the front lines.

▶ A simple way to look at authenticity is to see it as writing your own story. Each time you appear on video you're unveiling a new chapter.

▶ Being authentic doesn't mean sharing everything about yourself or exposing all of your vulnerabilities. You can share a side of yourself that is most appropriate for the context.

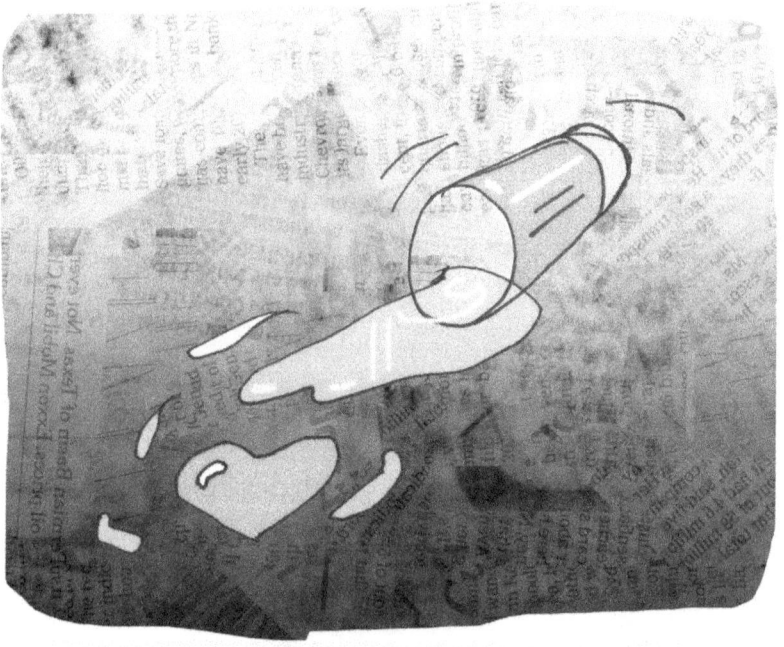

3

Nobody Wants Perfect

King George VI was on to something when he chose to lead as his authentic, imperfect self. Decades later, Brené Brown, a public speaker, researcher, and professor at the University of Houston, has made it her life's work to study vulnerability.[1] Brown posits that courage and speaking from the heart are one and the same. She put it this way in her TED Talk: "The original definition of courage, when it first came into the English language [comes] from the Latin word *cor*, meaning heart. And the original definition was to tell the story of who you are with your whole heart."

Out of the thousands of people she's studied, Brown discovered that those who displayed courage were willing to let go of who they thought they *should* be in order to *be* who they *were*. They had the courage to be imperfect.[2]

King George VI's speech supported Brown's point well before its time. When Bertie gave his speech in the dark days before WWII, the only man in the room was his voice therapist, Lionel Longue. As the story is told in the film *The King's Speech*, Lionel brought up some stumbles, "You still stammered on the W," to which the king replied, "I had to throw in a few so they would know it was me."[3] Everyone in the British Empire knew the king stuttered. How better to assure them this was really the king speaking from his heart? By embracing his vulnerabilities he showed his courage—a quality that colored every one of his actions as a leader.

To be real, you need to let down your guard to let your true self get out. That's not easy for many leaders. Many people at the top are used to being in control of every fact and figure. They equate making mistakes with weakness, especially on camera. In reality, showing our flaws can motivate people to listen *more* closely to what we have to say. Making mistakes, showing some emotion, or poking a little fun at ourselves can validate that we're speaking from the heart instead of a script.

When I direct leaders, I'm helping them transmute vulnerable feelings so they can use them creatively. When leaders display anxiety, I tell them to think of anxiety as being "excited" not "afraid." There's nothing wrong or weak about embracing your vulnerability, especially on camera.

One client was appearing on a video to explain a complicated corporate restructuring to her employees. She knew employees would wonder if the sea change would impact their jobs, and before we began to film she admitted to me that she didn't have all the answers.

She wanted to speak from the heart and show her concern about the welfare of her people.

This CEO took pride in being seen by her people as an authentic leader, and I reminded her of this. Why not just tell them (carefully, and with the approval of the communication and legal teams) the truth? On video she did just that. She said she didn't have *all* the answers yet (the truth), but when she got them her people would be the first to know (expressing care and concern). She said she was working with senior leadership to get answers as fast as possible (a promise that she eventually kept), and she gave them a date by which she'd have the answers.

This leader simultaneously showed vulnerability and respect for her people. By saying she was "on it," a problem-solving phrase she was used to hearing from her staff, the CEO projected some humility too. She knew she'd shared a truth: She didn't know everything.

Building authenticity requires revealing some vulnerability and in the process—some courage. Simply getting up in front of a camera makes us vulnerable and therefore shows courage. Admitting we're not perfect and telling a story about that fact takes courage. We all have anecdotes we can share in a measured and truthful way based on real experiences. Communicating these thoughts with others reveals our values and humanity and draws our audience closer.

Sharing vulnerability is a little scary, but feeling the fear and pushing ahead anyway pays off. With each video you make, each time you speak from the heart, your confidence on camera grows even if you stumble or fall now and then. And your story as a genuine, human leader continues to unfold.

"When a leader shows vulnerability and sensibil-
ity and brings people together, the team wins."

—HOWARD SCHULTZ

LEARNING BY FALLING DOWN

The path to speaking from the heart, especially on video, is similar to when you were a child learning how to walk. You pull yourself up off the floor, take a step or two, and fall on your butt. Urged and encouraged by your parents, you get up again and again.

Learning to walk is not about being judged for your stumbles and falls. If that were the case, we'd all be walking to the office on all fours. Falling down and getting up again is learning. Learning happens in an environment where vulnerability and courage thrive. This is the kind of environment I try to create as a director.

I've now directed the CEO of a major pharmaceutical company many times since his first video appearance. The first time, he was uncomfortable and awkward. He was the child who falls down. If I (or his staff) had criticized his performance, I don't think he would have stepped in front of a camera again. I've seen how good he is talking person-to-person and I've worked closely to help him translate that humanity to his on-camera performance.

We worked with him multiple times, so when it came to his most important announcement about a huge acquisition, he was ready. However, he arrived on set exhausted after an eighteen-hour day, just off the corporate jet from London. I don't think he was even sure what time zone he was in. And then we stuck him in front of a camera to rally thousands of new employees with a rousing message. A lot was at stake. The company had just spent tens of billions of dollars to buy a competitor. He was aware that he was introducing himself to over 22,000 new employees at the same time he was reassuring his current workforce about the wisdom of the merger. It was a big opportunity to put his leadership qualities on display and make a positive impression.

Part of his job was to enumerate the facts and figures of the merger. To convey the statistics properly was important. But beyond those details, his real mission was to convey his own passion and vision. He had to speak from the heart and punch through his fatigue.

The CEO welcomed the team from the acquired company and parlayed his excitement and warmth into a real *We*. "We're big in oncology, we're big in diabetes, and the new company will devote over $1 billion to research." I noticed his corporate communication executive perk up as he watched the presentation.

The CEO's enthusiasm for what was happening with his company and his knowledge of the subject shone through. But what really carried the presentation was the practice he had put into becoming himself in the moment and authentically portraying his emotions. That is what resonated with his employees. Regardless of the constraints he had been under, regardless of his fatigue, he was eloquent and true. It took him practice in front of the camera and a few pointers along the way to get there.

Remember: Your tribe isn't looking for a polished pro. They just want to get to know the elusive figure at the top. I had a conversation at a wedding a while back where a friend told me about how he'd watched his CEO grow up on-screen at corporate events. At first, the guy was awkward. He was petrified, and it showed in his performance.

But guess what? His people didn't mind. My friend pointed out that he didn't expect the CEO to be a movie star—he just appreciated that the guy took the time to connect with employees and share his message. Now, a decade later, that leader is much more comfortable on camera. He gets in front of the lens, casts his vision, and inspires action. My friend feels like he knows the CEO—and they've never even met!

Great leaders are usually good in person. But when you can't be there in person, you may feel stress about whether you can still make that critical connection. This concern can make some leaders nervous because they're placing so much importance on the video. And the video *is* important, but it's also important to cut yourself a break. There's a lot of latitude out there. There's a lot of empathy. Don't strive for perfection—strive for excellence. And remember that being authentic on camera is a journey. You're learning each time you make a video and each time you reveal another chapter of your story.

It's OK to stumble and fall, even on camera. Many strong leaders equate making mistakes with weakness. The counterintuitive reality is that our flaws can motivate people to listen more closely to what we have to say, according to Tina Orlando, a corporate communication expert and partner at the communication strategy firm, Indelable.

"One leader had a bit of a stutter and he'd get very anxious about it and I'd say, 'Look, people see you as the master of the universe and half of them are terrified of you. Every now and again when you make a little stumble or you do something that's human, it's actually very endearing to people. Think about it as your way of disarming them.

You're allowing them in to see you in a way that makes you more relatable. So don't worry so much about it.' Just trying to neutralize things like that and give people a slightly different perspective about it can help"[4]

Some leaders assume they can be good at everything they do from the first time they do it. When a CEO stumbles on a word, they often interrupt filming to say something like, "Sorry, I'll get it right next time." That isn't the point. If they are new to the game, I don't expect the next take will be much better. I know they are just beginning to walk so it's OK to fall down. I try not to stop CEOs when they stumble on a word or two. I let them get their footing and get through a whole take, then go back and work on smoothing out mistakes later if needed.

How could someone attempting something he or she has never done before—a craft that professionals devote their entire lives to mastering—expect to get it right on the first try? Tiger Woods learned to play golf when he was in diapers; he would never assume anyone could just step up to a tee and hit a hole in one. Meryl Steep would never think that she had to be "perfect" on take one. It doesn't matter how great a communicator you are in person. A great deal of work goes into a great video performance, and nobody expects you to be perfect.

The aim of this book is not to teach you how to be an actor, or how to give a great speech. Those are entirely different things. My goal is to show you how to be yourself on camera so you can bring your vision and important messages to life. But your authenticity won't show up on-screen until you're real with yourself offscreen. You can only do that by setting perfection aside.

In his memoir *Open*, tennis legend Andre Agassi highlights advice that fellow tennis player Brad Gilbert gave him about his game. Gilbert viewed perfection as a *sometimes thing*.

> Quit going for the knockout. Stop swinging for the fences. All you have to be is solid. When you chase perfection, when you make perfection the ultimate goal, do you know what you're doing? You're chasing something that doesn't exist. You're making everyone around you miserable. You're making yourself miserable. Perfection? There's about five times a year you wake up perfect, when you can't lose to anybody, but it's not those five times a year that make a tennis player. Or a human being, for that matter."[5]

> "Anyone who has never made a mistake has never tried anything new."
>
> **—ALBERT EINSTEIN**

Making mistakes and showing emotion will validate that you're a real, honest leader who is worth following. Because—remember—every time you appear on video, you're revealing another piece of your story. Do you want yours to be the story of a mouthpiece stuck in a suit? Or do you want it to be the story of an imperfect, passionate human who cares about her people? I'll let you guess which story your tribe wants to hear.

Nobody Wants Perfect—Key Ideas

▶ Building authenticity requires letting our guard down a little to reveal some vulnerability and in the process—some courage.

▶ Give yourself a break. It's OK to stumble and fall. Your audience doesn't want perfect. They just want to know that you care enough about them to reach out and connect. And remember that great editing can do wonders.

▶ Our flaws can motivate people to listen more closely to what we have to say.

4

The Sacred Space

If the idea of stepping in front of a camera and being real sounds hard, you're right. Actors spend their careers learning how to do it well, and those who have mastered it are considered legends. So, how can you be expected to do it within just a few minutes, often with no prep time at all?

The truth is, you can't. At least, you can't do it on your own. And you shouldn't have to.

Deep, honest communication can only come through in an atmosphere of trust and respect. I call this atmosphere the "sacred space," and it exists between you and your director. The sacred space is a safe environment where you sort out your message together and work closely to impart your humanity and authenticity on camera. It's where you and your director interact to convey your vision in a way that connects and sticks with the viewer.

Hollywood director and practicing Buddhist Peter Werner introduced me to the concept of the sacred space many years ago. He believes that of all the elements that go into a project, what happens in the sacred space is paramount. "With all the activity on a typical film set, all the technical gear, the noise, the sprawl, the people running around setting up lights, you can sometimes forget that the most important activity is often incredibly intimate: It's happening in a small space between maybe only two people, two actors, or the director and an actor. And it's the director's job to hold that space in the middle of the chaos, to allow for that connection to happen." Perhaps that's why he's been nominated for multiple Emmy and Director's Guild of America awards and has won an Oscar.

When you step in front of the camera, we're asking you to do something vulnerable and revealing. Actors are trained consistently over years to learn how to block everything out and maintain that trusted vibe with their director. It's the only way they can reveal their character to viewers in the most human way possible. The sacred space lets them remove the barrier between them and the lens.

It's only in corporate filmmaking that we treat this space so cavalierly. Leaders are expected—and expect themselves—to express their humanity on command. My peers who direct feature films, documentaries, and commercials always have at least one conversation with their actors so they can forge a connection. Movie stars meet with directors to see if they have a rapport. If they don't bond, the actor often won't do the film. But corporate leaders rarely get time to meet with their director in advance. As a top executive in your company, you're essentially playing a role every day. Your demanding job likely doesn't leave much room for your personal side to shine through.

Then you show up on set and are asked to take off the mask and *just be yourself.* It won't happen without trust. You can't be expected to deliver an honest performance without developing even the faintest rapport with your director.

Sometimes I need to create a sacred space almost instantly with someone who can't meet me until minutes before the camera rolls. I faced this challenge when filming the CEO of one of the fastest growing tech companies in Silicon Valley. He arrived on set late and I could immediately tell he expected to be treated like royalty because he had three personal handlers with him.

One of the ways I prep for a shoot is by observing what a leader wears in photos on his or her company website. This particular CEO wore a coat and tie, so I did the same on film day. When the leader arrived fifteen minutes late wearing an open-collar shirt, the first thing he said to me was, "Doesn't that tie cut off the circulation to your brain?" I kept my cool and simply said, "If you feel that way, you might want to change the photo on your website because you're wearing a tie in it." I didn't bristle or get defensive. In fact, I paired my reply with a warm chuckle to let him know I was on his side, even if I was pushing back on his comment.

Whether the CEO realized it or not, his tie comment was a test. He wanted to see what I was made of so he could figure out how much of himself he would be willing to give to me. He was gauging whether I was the kind of guy he could trust. This goes back to the concept of mirror neurons that I mentioned earlier. As the director, if I want the person I'm working with to be honest and open, I have to project that same vibe.

It's only natural to want to know you're in good hands, especially when you're about to venture into unfamiliar territory. Jim Tusty compares the experience to working with a coach. He points out that the last thing the CEO wants is to be in the hands of a Little League coach. They want the major league coach. The director has to convey their own authenticity and confidence if they want to build trust.[1]

The CEO instantly relaxed because he could tell I was someone who was willing to talk straight to him. I was confident and honest—traits that I hoped he'd bring to the camera. In a world full of yes men, he knew he could trust me to tell him the truth. He was ready to get to work.

Directors have to find a way to make these quick connections, sometimes in just a couple of minutes. Our job—and your performance—depends on it. Sometimes it happens by kindly speaking truth to power, as I did with my client in Silicon Valley. It's about being warm while showing that you're a strong person who is comfortable in his or her role.

A PARTNER TO BREAK THE TENSION

We've all seen movie outtakes or bloopers. They're a great window into understanding the atmosphere that needs to be present on a film set. Performers have to stay loose and in the moment. When someone messes up, they laugh. When someone really messes up, everyone laughs. They get through their blunders by not being so uptight. They acknowledge what happened and move on. In the same vein, if a CEO doesn't laugh or make light of a mistake, everyone gets rigid. You can hear a pin drop in the room.

In these moments, the person safeguarding the sacred space—usually the director—will often sacrifice his or her good standing to save the situation. Sometimes this means going against what the CEO or communications team said they wanted and instead doing what the project actually needs. If the speaker is tense, the director might clear the room for a relaxed one-on-one talk. Other instances might call for riskier moves.

A few years ago I was directing the CEO of the most valuable company in the world at the time. The guy was understandably busy, and always rushed. My team was given one hour to film a high-stakes video announcement for the company. A project of this caliber usually needs several hours, but an hour was all they would give us—or so I thought.

When we arrived on film day our slot had been cut to thirty minutes. We had no choice but to jump right into filming. After one take, the leader said he was done. He didn't have time for more, and anyway, he felt he'd delivered what was needed. This one rushed take was nowhere near enough, and I could tell his team knew it. But nobody was willing to rock the boat by speaking up. They were too afraid to piss off the boss.

I knew I was the expendable one in the scenario. While others in the room may have feared for their job, I knew I'd still have my business if the client decided he didn't want to work with me. I'd rather push back in the moment so I can deliver an excellent video than be complacent and make a lackluster video. So I put my good standing with the CEO on the line. I told him we needed more. He was noticeably irritated, but I persisted. I explained that what we had was OK, but the video would be even better with a few more takes because his passion hadn't come through in the material we had. He realized I was right. As I continued talking about a few things we could try, he inched away from the door and back into the room. It became clear he wasn't going to fire me. Instead, he'd decided to trust me.

You could feel the tension in the room break as the CEO settled in to shoot the next take. Our newly formed rapport allowed the conversation to flow more freely, and with that, the leader's performance was much more natural. With the sacred space firmly in place, the rest of the shoot took only an extra twenty minutes.

B-ROLL'S WELCOMED BY-PRODUCT

Taking a leader out to film B-roll before we shoot any speaking parts is a great way to establish trust before we ever step on set. It allows him or her the chance to become familiar with the crew, the camera, and me without the pressure of being "on." All they have to do is make-believe the crew and I aren't there.

Shooting B-roll is also the perfect way to introduce a leader to the filming process in general. My team is careful to praise good work and spontaneity during the sessions, and this helps our subject build confidence almost immediately. They begin to see that being on camera can feel natural.

When we shot B-roll of Becton Dickinson CEO Vince Forlenza, his comfort level rose almost immediately. Vince enjoys working with his leadership team, so we decided that putting them all together in a meeting might show off his confidence and ease with his colleagues.

"It was a lot of fun for me. You put me in a situation that I liked being in, interacting with a leadership team, with a group, doing Q&A. It really was helpful for me. In doing that B-roll, you get used to being on camera. And that's the other part of becoming more comfortable."[2]

Often, someone I'm filming can have better, more natural B-roll scenarios in mind than I do. I'm grateful to hear about and act on them. If we have done our job they tell us, "Hey this isn't so hard. I should be the director."

WORKING WITH THE TRUSTED TEAM

An important point I highlight is that we're all working toward the same goal—we just have different jobs. My role is to create a bond with the speaker and help bring out their best communication style. I help sharpen the message, make sure the body language is right, and that the leader's personality comes through. I can only do this if I've made a personal connection with the speaker and he or she understands that I have their best interests in mind. Everything I do is to help the organization achieve their desired outcome—whether it's getting stakeholders excited about a big company change or inspiring consumers to see their brand in a new light. My rapport with leaders will help keep them focused on their core goal in the midst of all the hubbub going on around the set.

The communications team, by contrast, helps make sure we've covered all the right points. I count on them to tell me if we've missed mentioning an important detail, or if the message is saying what it really needs to say. Their input is critical, but to do my job well I need one-on-one time with the leader. Time constraints sometimes force me to ask others to leave the filming area so I can set the right vibe quickly. It doesn't mean I don't want the team's input—I just need to create the right environment in which their input can be most effective.

I'll often set up a monitor off to the side, or in a nearby room, so the leader's team can see what's happening. I request that they let me ask the interview questions so I can build a rapport with the leader. The human rhythm that develops during a one-on-one interaction gives me a chance to ask the same questions in different ways to help the leader deepen his or her thinking on the subject. I promise to regroup with the team between takes so they can share their input. This keeps well-meaning colleagues from shouting out their feedback during filming. It's natural to want to do this, but I've found that when it happens the leader starts looking off camera and over at their colleagues for approval. It's hard to edit around these side glances, and at worst, it dilutes the sacred space and builds tension.

Klaus Schiang-Franck, owner of the film company Citizen Dane, also vies for one-on-one time with the speaker before filming. He often starts a shoot by asking the leader to tell him, without looking at a script, what he or she is going to talk about. Klaus says that when he does this, "You can see that this complicated thing can be explained so easily. They just tell me the story in a fraction of the time it would have taken to read it from a script. I encourage them to be short and precise, and they really like having the chance to just sit down and explain the story. It builds their confidence." In these moments Klaus makes sure nobody else is in the room. If someone on the communications team asks to participate, Klaus explains that he'd like this to be one-on-one time. If someone really wants to be involved, he asks them to take a role similar to his own: Stand back, don't say anything, and let the leader tell the story in his or her own words.[3]

Many people in corporate communication don't have a theater or film background. (If you're a corp comm pro *with* this experience, you have an edge on your peers!) That means the sacred space is often a foreign concept to anyone who isn't on the film crew, and it takes some explaining. Some leaders have an in-house comrade who makes it his or her job to preserve the sacred space. At American Express, Bob Florance holds the intriguing title of VP, Executive Electronic Communications. Bob is a CEO's dream at American Express and was at the other blue-chip companies he's worked with because it's his job to help executives get the right stuff on video and stop the wrong stuff from ever happening. A huge part of this job is guarding the sacred space. If you're lucky enough to have an experienced video person or director on staff, he or she can perform the dual function of making sure you're great on camera as well as ensuring that you're telling your story—and the company story—effectively.

Bob recalls one video shoot in his prior career as a director where he had to ask an influential corp comm executive to leave the room. The CEO being filmed was struggling to get his message right while the executive kept chiming in, saying, "It's no big deal, just say a few words and we'll be done with this." Bob had an intimate connection with the CEO and knew he didn't trust that particular colleague, which made it difficult enough to have the guy in the room. On top of that, the executive's impatient comments were zapping any hope of maintaining a supportive atmosphere on set.

Bob delicately asked the executive and a few other individuals to leave. They weren't happy about it because they felt their presence was critical to the video. But Bob had no choice. The video would be a flop if he didn't reclaim the sacred space with this CEO.

Once everyone was gone, Bob had a one-on-one talk with the leader to rebuild their trust and connection. They resumed filming with only the director and crew in the room. With nobody pressuring him to "get on with it," the CEO was able to deliver a heartfelt message in just a few takes.[4]

I've worked with Bob for years, at several companies, and it's amazing to witness his attention to detail when it comes to getting the job done right. He's extremely aware of what needs to happen and is not worried about throwing himself under the bus in the process. For Bob, it's all about building trust and integrity with the CEO he is there to support, and that trust is earned over time. Sometimes it involves asking an opinionated corp comm or PR person to leave the room during a shoot. Other times it means discreetly passing a tissue to a CEO so he can wipe his brow before going on camera.

It certainly helps to have someone like Bob on your side, whether they're part of your communications team or another trusted associate. But don't worry if you don't have such a dedicated copilot. A good director's first priority will be to establish a warm connection with you upon your first meeting.

Also take note if you're reading this as a member of your leader's support staff. It may not be your official job to foster the sacred space, but you can make yourself indispensible by stepping up to help bring warm vibes to a video shoot. This is because in business we often forget about the soft stuff. It's common for a leader's team to approach filming as if it's all about the words, not realizing their mind-set may inadvertently create a barrier that keeps the leader from being vulnerable or real. The sacred space is the only route to getting a true, human performance. Just knowing that the sacred space exists, and that it's vitally important, will help you do your part in kindling that connection. The director will thank you, and you may quickly become one of the most important people on your team for every video shoot.

I want to emphasize that the sacred space isn't fluff or theory. The insights in this chapter come from professionals who have worked with clients from the king and queen of Denmark to top executives at American Express, Coca-Cola, Pfizer, Raytheon, AT&T, and many others. The advice here is practical and proven, and if embraced, can transform your video appearances.

The Sacred Space—Key Ideas

- ▶ Deep, honest communication can only come through in an atmosphere of trust and respect.

- ▶ You can't be expected to deliver an honest performance without developing a rapport with your director.

- ▶ Movie bloopers are a great window into understanding the atmosphere that needs to be present on a film set. Performers have to stay loose and in the moment, and be willing to laugh at their mistakes.

- ▶ A good director's first priority will be to establish a warm connection with you upon your first meeting.

5

The Leader Has No Clothes

"A person's strength is to know their
weaknesses."

—RUSSELL SIMMONS

Most leaders won't be great on camera on their first try, and that's OK. There's a good reason why most companies have dedicated corporate communication departments—because solid communication takes skill, talent, focused work, and a great team. You're not expected to figure this out on your own, and hopefully you won't try to. If you're leading a major company, you'll likely have a PR or corp comm team to help you improve your video performances—that is, if you'll let them. But even if you don't have a dedicated department, it's worth listening to others' feedback and always being open as to how you can improve. Consider bringing in an outside coach if you truly don't have anyone to help you. It's important to have a trusted person to offer feedback on your video work, no matter how well you communicate off camera.

Your team will only be able to help you if they feel safe enough to offer constructive feedback without suffering any consequences. After all, how can you know if your performance could be stronger if no one feels they can tell you? You may *feel* authentic, you may *think* you're being true to yourself and the message, but perhaps everyone on set is biting their lips because they know you wouldn't take their feedback even if they tried to help you.

This chapter will help you build a supportive environment that encourages clear communication between you and your team. I also offer tips on the kind of language one should use when offering feedback on a performance. If you're a communications professional reading this book to help your leader improve his or her on-camera work, read on for advice on how to give feedback without bruising egos.

The operative word here is *feedback*. The goal isn't to criticize the performance, but to offer corrective feedback based on factual observations. As a leader, you need your confidants to communicate with you on this level. Even if you have a great relationship with your team, make sure they're offering the kind of objective feedback that I outline in this chapter. If they aren't, consider sharing these pages with them so they understand the vocabulary that will help you improve and that won't cause upset. That small act of openness alone will help strengthen the trust among your team.

The ability of others to give feedback, and for you to receive it, is critical. Because no matter how much of a natural you may be on-screen, you can always be better. Someone should be pointing out facets of your on-camera work that could use improvement. If your approach needs major work, the director (or someone on your team) should be taking you aside for a tactful heads-up. If that's not happening, you may have a bigger problem at play.

You may have inherited or created an environment that discourages feedback. If that's the case, your colleagues may feel uncomfortable telling you that you need to work on something as fundamental as your communication skills. After all, you've probably been speaking in public for decades and doing just fine. It's hard to suddenly tell the boss that he or she is not very convincing on camera. So no one dares to stir the pot. This is a dangerous place for you to be, especially if a lot is riding on your video. You may think you're dressed for success, but to others who hold their tongues, you're *buck naked*.

The Hans Christian Andersen tale *The Emperor's New Clothes* comes to mind. Written for children, it is a cogent analysis of CEO disconnects and, in case you don't remember the story, here are the crib notes.[1]

The emperor is a clotheshorse. He's all about image. He's so wrapped up in his image, the only thing he cares about is showing off his new outfits. Driven by vanity, he hires the best weavers in the land, who just happen to be two con men. They promise they can create clothes that are so uncommonly gorgeous they can only be seen by those who are fit to rule and smart enough for the office they hold. The new clothes he's offered are a two-for-one. Not only will the emperor look great, but he'll be able to spot all the dummies in his administration and let them go. Or will he?

When the "clothes" are finished, the rogues pantomime fitting them on the naked emperor. The monarch can't see them but won't admit it out of fear that *he* must be stupid and unfit to lead. The emperor's advisors follow suit (pun intended), as does the whole empire, save for one child who points out the emperor is nude. The emperor's people listen to the child. They know the boy's criticism is innocent and impartial, but by then it's too late to make things right.

Just like the emperor, any leader who makes his people feel foolish for stepping up and telling the truth can end up looking like the biggest fool in the room. If you're imperious, you'll never hear feedback. But here's the good news: Any leader reading this book probably doesn't fall into this camp. Or at least, your problems aren't as extreme as the emperor's. You wouldn't have picked up a book about improving your performance if you already thought you were great. You have a certain level of self-awareness, and that quality probably trickles down to the environment you've created in your company. If this is you, you're on the right track, but you may still have work to do before your team will be completely honest about your on-camera appearance.

If you have hired good communications people and created a work environment where they are encouraged to give you feedback, you are on the road to being a better you on camera. They know your personality and what you are up against day to day. All they need to help you is a little trust. Sound familiar? It's not unlike the sacred space. In this case, you want the bond to permeate through your whole team.

TRUST BUILT ON EMPATHY

Often the need for a leader to get in front of a camera comes up suddenly. In situations like these, leaders can feel exposed, defensive, or stressed out. Former Senior VP of Corporate Affairs at Allergan Charlie Mayr calms the waters by showing empathy for his boss.[2] He starts by listening to his boss's concerns and truly hearing what the issue is, then doing his best to address those concerns. This action builds the kind of trust that allows constructive feedback.

If you're working to help a leader fix his performance, your first step is to establish that trust with him. Even if you already have a great relationship, you may need to offer a few extra doses of empathy to remind him that you're a trustworthy comrade in this alien environment. When someone trusts you, they listen to your feedback. CEOs are familiar with using multisource feedback to evaluate and enhance performance throughout their organizations. Leaders should have the same regard for feedback on their video performances. But in my experience, many leaders designate video critiques a no-fly zone, and their advisors let them get away with it since filming video is such foreign territory for all involved. It's even worse if the leader has made it clear, either directly or through disgruntled behavior, that he or she hates being on camera.

"Love all, trust a few, do wrong to none."

—WILLIAM SHAKESPEARE

Everyone can get through this with a little trust, and it requires full participation from both sides of this equation. Both leaders and advisors must form strategies that are positive and empowering. But it's the leader who must get the ball rolling by believing that his team is on his side.

As a leader you have to trust the obvious: What reporting person would go out of their way to offer feedback without any basis in fact? If that same person told you that there was a discrepancy in an end-of-year report, or that a pitch going out to a major client still needed work, would you doubt them? Probably not. Because you hired this person to bring their insight and expertise to the company. Any feedback they offer in their role is with the purpose of helping the company get ahead. Why would their feedback on your performance be any different?

When directing a leader who flubs on camera, I try to keep his or her frustration level down any way I can. I once told one executive, "No great actor learned the craft overnight; why should you?" When I cut him that slack, his performance improved. But serious improvement requires the right kind of feedback.

> "He who closes his ears to the views of others shows little confidence in the integrity of his own views."
>
> **—WILLIAM CONGREVE**

NO PLACE FOR CRITICISM

Trust among colleagues is golden, but it takes more than trust to help you improve on camera. Everyone involved must understand that the dialogue is one of *feedback*, not criticism. There's a big difference between the two. Nobody likes to be criticized. Criticism is almost always subjective and therefore it's perceived negatively because we feel like we are being judged based on someone's personal interpretation of our work. Feedback, by contrast, is entirely objective. It's not interpretable. It's not about judging the person or their performance; it's merely an observation of the facts that can be seen by anyone with the movie camera.

Ultimately, giving feedback requires us to change our vocabulary at every stage—from prep sessions to film day. To do that, look for the facts that everyone can agree on and discuss them objectively. For example, if you think the speaker sounds angry, it doesn't help to simply say, "You sound angry." Drill down to the action that is giving off the angry vibe and try to highlight moments that worked. You could say something like, "You raised your voice. The tone you used when describing the new widget to me earlier worked really well."

If the person on camera is slouching, it won't help much to say, "You look sloppy," but try, "The way you were sitting makes you look like you are too relaxed for the seriousness of your message."

It's much easier—and effective—to give and receive feedback when the conversation revolves around the facts. These dialogues can take place among the leader and the support team during prep, or even on set when the director asks colleagues to share their thoughts.

LEADERS, EMBRACE FEEDBACK

If you're fortunate enough to work for a leader who values feedback, it's vital to give the kind of objective feedback I just described. If you're the leader on the other side of the camera, remember that your trusted advisors are there to help you improve. Ignoring feedback can set up some harsh lessons for leaders who think they're infallible. Jon Pepper, partner and cofounder of the New York–based communication strategy firm Indelable, learned this over the course of his thirty-year career.

"It's so easy to fall into the trap where you begin to think you're special. If you're a CEO, you *are* special. But that doesn't mean you're beyond learning and receiving constructive guidance from the people you've hired to help you. I think the best CEOs are those who are willing to have their thinking challenged constantly and who consider those kinds of challenges in the spirit in which they're given."[3]

I would add that accepting feedback has a ripple effect. It empowers your team, helps you shine on camera, gets your videos seen, and makes your organization more successful.

Just remember—as you improve on camera, don't let your ego get in the way of striving to be even better. Keep asking for feedback, keep the channels open. Go as far as choosing a few key people to review your videos and encourage them to freely give you feedback on your performances. Keep your ego in check even if people are telling you how wonderful you are as a boss on and off camera.

Leaders who have reached the pinnacle can tend to believe their own press. They have a sense of invincibility. Jon Pepper points out that with little or no serious feedback coming their way, they take on all the trappings of wealth and power.[4] Even when they hurtle off the rails, they still have a sense of invulnerability. We are all driven by vanity and ego in varying degrees. High-powered leaders can be driven by these forces in the extreme. In the business world this malady is known as CEO Disease (CEOD).[5]

CEO DISEASE

The term CEO Disease was coined by an executive vice president of a *Fortune* 500 company. He was so worried he'd catch CEOD himself that he assembled a cadre of advisors to warn him if he began to exhibit any of the symptoms. He really wanted people to tell him if he *had no clothes*.

One of the most insidious characteristics of CEOD is that the sufferers are blind to how their moods and actions affect the people in their organization. They also incorrectly assume they can decipher their shortcomings themselves. Even worse—they think if they are screwing up, someone will tell them so. But when bosses proclaim themselves masters of the video universe, it's hard for the corp comm people to say, "You actually need a lot of work on your camera persona." And this issue goes way beyond videos. If CEOD stymies filming, it's probably infecting other areas of the company as well.

So what to do? Well, you can't change the company culture overnight, but you can leverage some strategies to at least improve the video situation. The advice that follows speaks to people who are trying to help their leader improve his or her performance, since those infected with CEOD will be too oblivious to know it. But leaders, take note. If it seems your team is tiptoeing around you, maybe you need to look in the mirror. Keep reading, since you'll be an active participant in the feedback loop.

TRY A LITTLE PRACTICE AND PLAYBACK

Mitigate your boss's defensive resistance to your feedback by suggesting that with "a little more work and practice," the boss could be even greater than he thinks he already is. Jon Pepper at Indelable reviews past videos with executives to encourage them to practice on-camera skills and analyze elements like tone of voice, eye direction, and body language.

> I think the most effective way to get them to prac-
> tice is to show them the results on video. Executives
> are typically bright people. If they can see how they
> come across on camera, they may change their mind
> in terms of how effectively they think they've done and
> how much preparation is required.[6]

This is exactly what the best athletes do by reviewing their game-day footage. This kind of approach can work wonders, and later on in the book I'll devote an entire chapter to preparation and practice.

SERVE THE MEDICINE ON A SUGAR CUBE

One of the best ways to channel feedback is to buffer it with a little praise and positivity. When corporate communication expert Tina Orlando works with leaders, she emphasizes the positives during her shoots. "I will never go into the negative in an interview," Tina says. "I always frame it in the positive and say, 'Hey, you remember when you did this? Let's do a little bit more of that because that worked really well and that's just what we want.'"[7]

Like Tina, I help leaders on camera by coming at problems from nonthreatening angles. If their energy on camera begins to flag, I might suggest they raise the volume of their voice. Often this gets the juices flowing without their feeling deficient in some way.

BEWARE OF MEDIA TRAINING

I've met hundreds of CEOs, presidents, and leaders in my career, and most of them are dynamic type-A men and women. They have no problem standing in front of a large crowd and delivering a captivating speech. But that inspiring persona somehow evaporates the minute you put a camera lens near them. Why?

I believe it has something to do with control. A CEO is the big kahuna. The Boss. They're used to being in charge. And then they get on a film set with a director, a producer, and some assistants, and all of a sudden all eyes are trained on them in a strange situation.

So what do they do? They fall back on one trusty tool—media training. But that's the exact wrong response, because while media training prepares you for some specific situations, it can suck all the authenticity out of you and leave nothing but a corporate talking head. It teaches people to pivot, to avoid, to squirm, and to dodge. Media training helps people go on Fox News or sit with Charlie Rose or get in a good quip at the debate, but what happens in media training is the total opposite of what it takes to be *you* on camera. Viewers don't want a polished sound bite machine. They want a real human.

Personal branding expert Russell Amerasekera has often had to untrain executives who were taught to go on the offensive at the first sight of a camera. "I'm quite a cynic about media training," he says. "The whole process is often based around filling the person that's going through it with fear."[8]

Media training has its place, of course. It can keep you from looking foolish when a smug reporter asks you a gotcha question. But that's live TV. When we put a leader on camera, we don't want her to turn away. We want her to face us. We want her to lean in. We want her to trust that we're taking time to craft a story together, and we'll piece it all together carefully, in the editing room, like a work of art. If you notice that the leader you're working with falls back on media training, it's worth taking her aside to point out these differences. If you're the one in front of the camera, take note. You don't need to lean on the defense mechanisms that media training may have engrained in you. You're not on live TV trying to dodge probing questions. You have complete control over your message, and nobody will see the video until you're completely happy with it.

Media training won't help improve your video work, but on the bright side, improving your video performances can help with your media appearances. Think about it: The more comfortable you are in front of the camera, the less likely you are to pivot and squirm during your next media appearance. You can just be *yourself*.

BRINGING IN AN OUTSIDE CONSULTANT

Some leaders believe that outside communication consultants are better able to give them unvarnished criticism compared to staff who may be more of the yes men variety. Professional consultants can offer an honest evaluation to leaders without worrying about consequences. That's what they are paid to do, after all.

Consultants are expendable and they know it. Taking a bullet for delivering an unpopular message is a consultant's job. The outside consultant is the little boy who pointed out the emperor had no clothes. It's not a perfect solution, but hearing the feedback from an outside expert can break the ice both for leaders and their advisors.

DIRECTORS

Research and vet directors carefully. You want to find someone who will work with you to help you deliver your best possible performance. Take the time to talk to them and ask how they help clients figure out the best video format for their personality and message. You need to have great chemistry with your director, and part of that requires the director to be honest, warm, and flexible. As a director, I'm kind of a hybrid consultant, but only in the moment. During the shoot, I make it clear that my job is to help the leader be his or her best self on camera. I'm there to get the job done on the designated day and not do a job on anyone. The more time I can get with leaders to get to know them, the more I can help in the span of shooting time I'm allowed.

I've felt the fear and frustration of corp comm people and other advisors who would bend over backward to help their leader, if only they were invited. I've met leaders who honestly recognize they're failing on camera but won't reach out for help because they fear looking weak. Tear down that wall.

The Leader Has No Clothes— Key Ideas

▶ Your team can help you become more authentic on camera, but they need to know that you're open to their help. It's important to build trust among your team so they know they can offer feedback without suffering consequences.

▶ If you're working to help leaders improve their performance, remember that empathy builds trust. They will be more willing to accept your feedback if they feel you understand what they're going through.

▶ Remember: feedback, not criticism. Criticism feels personal, whereas feedback is merely an observation of the facts. Leaders, if your trusted advisors aren't offering the kind of objective feedback you need, share this chapter with them so they know what you're looking for.

▶ Beware of CEO Disease, a state of being blind to how your moods and actions affect the people in your organization.

▶ Make sure your director is willing to work with you to help deliver your best possible performance. When vetting directors, ask how they work with clients to deliver a great message.

PART II

STEPPING IN FRONT OF THE CAMERA

6

It's Not Just about the Words . . .

There's so much more to communication than the words we speak. Context, body language, and our tone of voice all work together to convey our message's true meaning. Consider the following scenario.

A couple was enjoying a romantic moment watching the sunset at the beach when the man put his arm around the woman's shoulders and said, "Life doesn't get any better than this." Months later, the same two people attended their daughter's wedding. After a year of planning, the night was going smoothly until the groom's ex-wife, drunk and belligerent, found her way to the reception. She yelled. She cried. She threw things. In the middle of her tirade, the same man crossed his arms, turned to his wife, and said, "Life doesn't get any better than this."

Same exact phrase, two very different meanings. Without the context of the scene (beach vs. drunk ex), you wouldn't understand the man's intended meaning. The words only count for a small portion of communication.

It's easy to get so caught up in *what* you'll say on camera that you forget to consider how your message is coming across to viewers. In addition to context, your facial expressions, eye movements, vocal intonation, and body language affect what you say more than the actual *words* you speak. Experts call these physiological signals non-verbals, and they're a major factor in whether others view you as a good person—both on camera and off.

Your non-verbals help validate your humanity; they communicate your trustworthiness and are just as important as the words you speak. Non-verbals are the physiological sinews that connect one heart to another. We all know great communicators when we hear them and especially when we *see* them. Often we can turn the volume off and a speaker's non-verbals inform us whether they are confident, whether they are comfortable, and whether they are honest.

Body language expert Mark Bowden helps us understand why non-verbals are so important. He explained in his TEDx talk that the primitive brain is wired to make snap judgments about others. The brain picks up signals from a person's non-verbal behavior to decide whether he is a friend, a predator, or whether we should be indifferent to him. Bowden goes on to explain that we're preprogrammed to be indifferent to others. By default, we won't pay attention to someone unless our brain has put him in the "friend" category. So unless your viewers already know and like you, their instinct is to not listen to you at all.[1]

Bowden reveals simple non-verbal behaviors that can quickly bump you into the "friend" spot before you speak a word. One simple gesture is to stand with your palms and your stomach open. This signals to others' primitive brains that you come unarmed. It also indicates that you don't consider the other person to be a predator, because you're willing to expose the area of your body that houses your organs. If you leave this area unprotected, others will subconsciously see you as an honest person who is good and safe to be around.

THE POWER OF A SMILE

"Smile in the mirror. Do that every morning and you'll start to see a big difference in your life."

—YOKO ONO

Your smile also plays a big part in getting you to friend status with your viewers. The primitive brain evaluates smiles. Bowden explains that we can't simply flash a quick, or toothy, smile. A smile must build for about three seconds, and last for just as long. It also needs to create wrinkles in the corners of your eyes. If your smile is insufficient, your viewers' brains will default to tossing you into the predator category. Bowden is referring to the *Duchenne smile*, the facial expression named after nineteenth-century French neurologist Guillaume-Benjamin Duchenne, who practiced medicine in the Boulogne-sur-Mer region of France. He was obsessed with facial expressions and believed they were gateways to the soul. Around 1862, he conducted experiments using electrical probes to trigger muscle reactions on patients' faces. He discovered that the presence or absence of eye-muscle contractions separate real smiles from forced and fake ones.[2] A genuine smile requires more than just turning up the corners of your mouth. The skin around the corners of your eyes has to crinkle like crow's feet. We now know that if this subtlety is absent in your smile, people will inherently mistrust you.[3]

To see a full-on Duchenne smile in action, check out the *TIME* magazine video interview with Virgin Group CEO Richard Branson on the web.[4] When a reporter asks him a series of questions about his life and philosophy Branson stumbles on his replies more than once, but you kind of don't care because his smile is pure Duchenne, especially when he jokes that he didn't understand the difference between gross and net profits until after a board member explained it to him. When asked about global warming, however, he becomes more somber and introspective. Not only does Branson have a genuine smile, he uses it appropriately and we read from his face that he is an authentic leader.

Inducing a real smile is not easy. Even the best actors know that, so some stars have learned to use mind tricks to summon up real smiles based on a real experience. I remember watching in awe as Meryl Streep smiled and laughed in *The Bridges of Madison County*. In an interview with Oprah Winfrey, Streep said she was able to smile convincingly by thinking about all the times that Clint Eastwood forgot his lines. Streep knew better than to fake it—instead she thought of something real that made her smile from the heart and not the brain.[5]

This technique worked for Streep when she had to place herself in a fictional role, but hopefully you won't be "acting" in your videos. The goal, as I've stressed, is to be yourself. But Streep's strategy can still help when you're struggling to *just be you* on camera. If you tend to tense up in front of the lens, remember Streep's trick and think of a personal anecdote or experience that makes you smile. Even better, try thinking of some of your best times at work, or whatever the topic of your video might be. If you're revealing year-end results, think of some moments of triumph that helped you get to where you are. Even if the numbers you're sharing aren't stellar, you probably had some great experiences with your colleagues as you worked together to achieve your goals. Think of positive experiences you may have had with some of your viewers. Simply doing this can help you relax and offer a genuine smile for the camera.

If you feel you don't have the time or brain space to think much about non-verbals, a quick focus on channeling your Duchenne smile using our Meryl Streep–inspired exercise can transform your on-camera appearance. The benefits are twofold, because once you tap a genuine smile you're more likely to relax and gain your viewers' trust.

ORGAN OF EMOTION

While Bowden's insights build on Duchenne's research, other recent findings further emphasize the power of our facial expressions. Using MRI imaging, neuropsychologists have discovered a complex network of specialized areas in the human brain that support our face-reading skills.[6] Our face gives our fears and insecurities away and can show whether we're speaking the truth.

The face has been called the "organ of emotion," and we depend on reading facial expressions to understand what others are feeling. We "encode" messages in our facial expressions, and we simultaneously "decode" the faces of the people around us. Phrases like "I could read the fear on his face" didn't come out of nowhere.

Our facial expressions impact our credibility, according to researchers. When someone tries to conceal his or her emotions, "leakage" of that emotion can be read in that person's face. The leakage may be limited to one region of the face (a mini or subtle expression) or may be a quick expression flashed across the whole face (a micro expression).[7]

They call University of California San Francisco professor Paul Ekman the Human Lie Detector. He can recognize thousands upon thousands of nearly imperceptible facial expressions that most of us ignore. They're called micro expressions, and you may have seen them in the short-lived TV series *Lie to Me* based in part on Ekman and his work.

Most recently, Ekman worked with director Pete Docter on his hit animated film *Inside Out*. Ekman and scientist Dacher Keltner helped Docter understand how emotions portrayed by his five main characters, Joy, Sadness, Disgust, Anger, and Fear, exist together in a person's mind.[8] And while scientists now study more emotions, those five key emotions (and a few others) are the main ingredients that combine to generate each of Ekman's micro expressions.

What's going on in the brain is seen on the face. And for those of us who make video content, and for those who go on camera, *Lie to Me* and *Inside Out* can teach us a valuable lesson.

When watching a CEO on camera, a company employee can, like a mini Ekman, intuitively read what's on his leader's face. If you come into your recording session with baggage from a bad day, that bad day will enter the communication, and even if you're reading a joyful script, your delivery will be colored with irritation no matter how hard you try to hide it.

I'm not suggesting you sugarcoat everything and become a master deceiver. In fact, the key lesson from *Inside Out* is that true joy can really only exist hand-in-hand with some bits of sadness. In screenwriting, storytellers get an emotional response not from playing one note but from varying their tune and hearing the harmonics that come with several notes. Life without variation is boring.

You might be announcing a merger to your company. It's natural and acceptable that there's a tinge of trepidation or fear of the unknown—as long as it's balanced by the excitement of opportunity and the courage to forge ahead. As a leader going on camera, you have to be thoughtful and purposeful about not only your message, but also exactly how you'll present it. Going on camera is intimate. Your face occupies thousands of pixels—and your audience will be able to intuit whatever is behind the words you say.

Whatever baggage you came with must be left at the door. If you ignore this important step, you'll undermine the very message you're trying so hard to communicate. Mark Bowden emphasizes this point in his TEDx talk. He explains that you have to choose your behaviors if you want others to listen to you, even if it means you're technically being inauthentic in the moment.[9] In other words, if you walk into your video shoot still angry from your morning meeting, you'll hurt your relationship with viewers if you behave authentically by showing that anger on-screen. You must choose the right behaviors. You want viewers to know that you're their friend, that you're on their side, and that you have their interests at heart.

USING BODY LANGUAGE THAT REFLECTS THE REAL YOU

Your non-verbals affect much more than your first impression on viewers. They help paint the broader picture of who you are as a person. As a director working with leaders, I'm more sensitive to body language than ever. If I'm given some quality time to hang out with a leader, I pay a lot of attention to their natural gestures. How do they normally sit? Are they leaning forward or sitting back? Do they cross their legs? What are they like when they are animated, talking normally, or laughing? I want to work with their natural style as much as possible, but sometimes the authentic ways they move their arms and head vanish when we start filming. Even worse, they replace these gestures with forced movements. Viewers quickly sense these gestures are contrived, and they begin to lose confidence in the message and interest in the video.

The camera has a way of exaggerating our movements if they are unnaturally animated. When I mentioned this phenomenon to Jon Pepper, he brought up an interesting dynamic: If you are an extrovert you can have a harder time on camera.

"You can look like a Jim Cramer, for instance, whose motions are entertaining to some but distracting to others and may get in the way of the message. Sometimes introverts play really well on camera because they tend to be more understated, a little cooler and less animated. A raised eyebrow can communicate more effectively than wildly swinging arms."[10]

Since video captures and exaggerates every movement—your eyebrow, your smile, a grimace—it's well worth your time to pay attention to these movements. Review your performances. Are you really gesturing and moving like you?

You can also use gestures and body language as a tool to increase your confidence on camera. Because of the way humans are wired, striking a certain posture can influence our mood positively, and this in turn helps engage viewers.

Amy Cuddy, a professor at Harvard Business School and sought-after body language expert, has remarked, "Non-verbals govern how other people think and feel about us." Like facial expressions, body language often cuts across cultures, genders, and physical disabilities. For instance, Cuddy notes that power and confidence are often indicated by expansive postures and gestures. When we feel powerless we tend to fold our arms and slink down in our chairs trying to make ourselves physically smaller.[11]

Paul Ekman's work and the insights shared by Amy Cuddy mirror some methods employed by accomplished actors. In biopics, actors study how subjects move and gesture. They do this not only to morph into these characters but also to feel like the people they are playing. You can use non-verbals to feel more like yourself.

Cuddy suggests that if you stand in front of a mirror and smile a real smile, you may notice you actually feel happier.[12] Try it sometime. Or strike the Wonder Woman (or Superman) pose—stand up straight with your hands resting on your hips. Do you feel small and out of control or confident and powerful?

I'm not advocating you embody comic book heroes the next time you communicate on camera. But by trying these two exercises I'm hoping you get a visceral sense of the power that facial expressions and body language can have in communication.

WORKING WITH YOUR DIRECTOR ON NON-VERBALS

A great director will help monitor your non-verbals and guide you toward the right moves. Before a shoot, I show my interviewee some gestures to indicate they may need to make some adjustments. I may place my index finger between my eyes to signal their eyes are straying or put a finger under my chin to indicate they need to raise their head or sit ramrod straight in my chair to urge them to also sit up straight. Aside from the fact that sitting up straight makes you more attentive to and respectful of your audience, it also changes your state of mind.

As a director, I've sometimes used my own tone and body language to influence the level of energy I'm trying to get out of an interviewee's performance. Bob Florance, of American Express, has used a similar approach.

"The person that you're interviewing often reflects your mannerisms and your intensity or lack of intensity," Bob explains. "If you talk in a quiet voice, they're going to do the same. So whatever you want to try to get from them, if you reflect those mannerisms, they'll often pick up on it."[13]

A director should also be monitoring his subject's breathing. At the gym, your trainer is always reminding you to keep breathing normally when you lift weights. Scuba divers can suffer embolisms if they hold their breath. When something is new or physiologically difficult, we tend to hold our breath. The same thing happens when we're a little anxious. You won't get embolisms if you hold your breath on camera, but if you try to blurt out an answer without letting yourself breathe you'll come off as scared and unnatural. Breathing naturally is what you do when you talk off camera. Breathing in and out also regulates the tempo of your words in a natural manner.

Your body language and facial expressions deserve your attention when you step in front of the camera. If you don't choose the right non-verbal behaviors, you may lose viewers before you even speak. Once you do begin talking, you may feel positive about the message, but your body language and facial expressions might indicate that you're not. The danger here is that viewers may assume you are uncomfortable with your message as well. As we'll see in a later chapter, taking time to review your work on video can help you see where your non-verbal behaviors are working against the authentic you.

It's Not Just about the Words— Key Ideas

- ▶ Your facial expressions, eye movements, vocal intonation, and body language affect what you say more than the actual *words* you speak.

- ▶ Channeling an authentic smile is a powerful form of warm, inviting non-verbal communication.

- ▶ When working on your on-camera non-verbals, try to maintain the natural posture you'd carry when talking to someone in person. A great director will help monitor your non-verbals and guide you toward the right movements.

7

Meet Your Film Crew

L et's face it: Acting naturally in front of a camera feels pretty, well, *unnatural*. The whole setup pulls you out of your comfort zone, and you're expected to just ignore the bright lights and be yourself. You've likely never experienced a world like this before, so it's bound to feel a little strange. Just imagine . . .

You return from lunch and head for the "set" as scheduled. This might be a boardroom or your own office. As you walk out of the elevator you start getting that "we're not in Kansas anymore" feeling. You spot a power cable duct-taped to the carpet and follow it down the hallway for your interview. The aliens await you at the other end.

When you walk through the door, it feels a little like coming home and finding Martian men moving into your house. You're confronted by lights and at least a half dozen strangers. Tables and desks are rearranged. The flowers you gave your assistant to celebrate her thirtieth birthday are now sitting on the windowsill next to a half-scale terra cotta warrior the crew has borrowed from the waiting area on the ground floor.

The camera lights are being tested and the room is a whole lot brighter and warmer. The shoot has been on your schedule for a few days, but only now does it sink in, in a visceral way, that it's show time—and *you're* the show.

You've got an important message and only so much time allotted to play your part. The good news is that everyone in the room is there to help you pull it off. In fact, the director, the film crew, and all that gear have only one purpose: to make you look and sound great on camera.

The only way to feel at home among this alien crew is to get to know them, so sit back and meet your team. But before we meet the *people* making your video, let's look at the one element in the room that probably gives you the biggest jitters—the camera.

NOT YOUR TYPICAL LOVE AFFAIR

The camera is just the collection point of any production, be it a multimillion-dollar feature or a home movie. The image that comes in through the lens and the recorded sound is simply "what's there." The camera is not an enemy to be overcome. You can't win by trying to outsmart the camera.

It's hard to *ignore* a camera, but it's a great goal to strive for. Great actors spend their entire careers learning to ignore the things.

Remember, the camera's job is to just record "what's there." If you learn to give a good delivery on video, the camera will embrace your performance like an awestruck groupie.

> ### "The camera loves you."
>
> ### —MICHAEL CAINE

The great screen actor Michael Caine personified the camera as someone who loves you no matter what.

> The first time you go out in front of a camera is not like going out on a first date. You don't have to make a special impression. The camera doesn't have to be wooed; the camera already loves you deeply. Like an attentive mistress, the camera hangs on your every word, your every look; she can't take her eyes off you. She is listening to and recording everything you do however minutely you do it; you have never known such devotion. She is also the most faithful lover while *you* for most of your career, look elsewhere and ignore her.[1]

But through the collective effort of those behind and in front of the camera, the editing process, and the addition of music, we can make "what's there" way greater than the sum of its parts.

A GOOD DIRECTOR

You may be the CEO of the most successful company in the world or president of the largest university, but when you appear on camera for the first time, it's normal to feel those newbie jitters. Best-selling author Bill George teaches several courses that CEOs attend at Harvard Business School. Bill told me that one of the top concerns among his CEO participants is dealing with the media and especially appearing on camera. These smart, successful executives know it's important for them to do it, but they also realize their experience may not be enough to prepare them for a great performance.[2] If you feel this way, you're not alone. Know that a good director senses your concern, reads your mood, and knows how to put you at ease. As discussed earlier, this is what the sacred space is all about.

Good directors should motivate and guide you. They understand that you are out of your element and likely to be uncomfortable. A good director should coax you into relaxing, encourage you to be yourself, and remind you to forget about being perfect. The more relaxed you are, the more powerful and truthful your narrative; and the more your message will reach your audience. Now you are ready for your first take.

When the director gives you the signal to begin speaking, it's the start of a "take." When the director indicates you can stop, or that the action can cease, that's the end of the take. You may grow irritated if a director asks you for another take or another run-through of your material. Remember that your director sees aspects of your performance that you don't. Trust his or her direction, even when it might mean doing more takes than you'd like.

Amateur or not, your instincts matter during a shoot. So if your director rushes you, doesn't try to make you more comfortable, or simply lets you do a few takes and then says good-bye when you think you could have done better, you should hire another director, one you trust.

Directing a top-level executive is about building trust and building it instantly in whatever thirty-minute (or shorter!) window a director may be given in a CEO's schedule. My job as a director is to listen to language, gauge pacing, and assess honesty. It's about acting as the "first audience" for the executive's message in order to anticipate how the *real* audience might react to his on-camera appearance. I am backed up by a highly skilled crew that, like me, make it their business to create as relaxed an atmosphere for the leader as possible on the set.

Good directors have solid, trusting relationships with the rest of the crew and depend on their input during all phases of shooting. If an airliner passes over the building while you're talking to the camera, for example, the director might ask the sound mixer if it's necessary to reshoot.

The first thing I do when the leader arrives for the shoot is introduce everyone in the crew. Some CEOs are such people persons that they beat me to the punch, but many others are trying to adjust to the alien world and may be feeling too anxious to stop and say hello.

Introductions not only help break the ice; they give me the opportunity to explain each person's role and expertise. I want the leader to know that I've chosen empathetic, friendly, and professional people for the shoot. I make it clear to the person on camera that this is not *any* crew—this is *their* crew. We're not there to judge them. We're there to make them look and sound as good as we possibly can.

FILM CREW ROLES

The crew's size for a corporate production depends on the scope of the work. In most cases, it consists of a director, producer, director of photography (DP), production manager (PM), a soundperson or "mixer," a lighting person, a makeup person, and a production assistant (PA). Some of these roles can double or triple if we have to film a CEO in two buildings or locations on a tight schedule. One crew needs to be "prepping" the second location while the other crew is shooting at the first location.

Here's a little more intel about our different roles and pecking order.

Producer

You've already met the head honcho on the shoot—the director. Next in line is the producer. In general, the producer looks at the big picture. He or she interfaces with your trusted advisors on the message and goals of your project. With these goals in mind, the producer may put together a list of questions that the director will put into play during an interview. If B-roll is needed, the producer will compile a shot list. Before the shoot, the producer will work closely with the director to make sure the client's objectives are crystal clear. Although the director has studied the questions to be asked in the interview, the producer is a backup, making sure that in all the rush, no questions are lost in the shuffle.

Director of Photography (DP)

For our purposes, this title is interchangeable with cameraman. I use the title DP because anyone can switch a camera off and on. A DP is also a lighting artist and more. A good DP uses the lights to shape your face in the most engaging way possible. During the shoot, the DP works closely to frame the shots in a way that best suits the tone of the video in concert with the director's vision.

Production Manager (PM)

This is the person who creates the shooting and production schedules, books flights and hotels, and coordinates the crew that's been selected by the director and/or the producer. The PM's domain includes everything from getting permissions and film permits to making sure the crew knows exactly where and when we cart our gear into the building.

Lighting Person

Like all industries, film has its own nomenclature that lets you know you're on the inside. For example, we call the lighting person a gaffer. Working closely with the DP, the lighting person selects, assembles, and roughs out the positions for the lights and reflectors. Depending on the complexity of a shoot, we may add a grip, who helps move equipment and set up stands. And the person who assists everyone on the lighting team is called the best boy.

Makeup

After I shake your hand and introduce you to the crew, your next point of physical contact is often the makeup artist. Their job is not to make you look "pretty"—it's to make you look natural on camera. He or she is also looking for anything on your face or person that could distract viewers from what you're saying, such as a flyaway hair, a blemish, or bags under your eyes from that twenty-four-hour merger negotiation. I always find makeup artists who are friendly conversationalists. They can help put you at ease as they dab some powder on your forehead or nose.

Production Assistant (PA)

While they are often the most junior person on set, good PAs have saved the day on many a shoot. Often they will pick up the crew at the airport, schlep our gear, and do whatever else needs to get done ASAP. We need them the most at the beginning and end of a day as we enter and leave a location. A good PA will sit off in a corner during the shoot like a fireman waiting to put out a fire. When there's too much noise in the hallway, the PA is the first one to slip outside to ask for quiet. Many PAs go on to become directors or producers. Some are now running networks and have become CEOs, or left the film business entirely and started their own venture capital firms. So be nice to PAs.

Meet Your Film Crew—Key Ideas

▶ Be choosy about the director you hire. A good director should motivate and guide you. He or she should be able to sense your discomfort, read your mood, and know how to put you at ease. They will honor the sacred space.

▶ Get to know your film crew. They're there to make you look and sound fantastic.

▶ The size of your crew will depend on the scope of the work. It typically consists of a producer, director, director of photography (DP), production manager (PM), a soundperson or "mixer," a lighting person, a makeup person, and a PA (production assistant).

8

Find Your Groove in Front of the Lens

One of the biggest decisions you'll make when planning a video is choosing your communication style. You have three broad options: speaking directly to the camera, speaking directly to an interviewer, or speaking directly to an audience. Each method has variations, which we'll explore in this chapter. The style you choose will depend on what you're most comfortable with, the message you're sharing, and most importantly, the amount of time you're able to devote to your communication. Whether you're filming in your company's in-house studio or firing up your laptop camera for a quick, intimate message, the concepts here still apply. Large-scale or small, the principles are universal.

Time to prepare with your director and communications team is the game changer when it comes to picking your most effective communication style. The more time you can put into preparing for film day, the more comfortable you'll feel in front of the camera, no matter what format you choose. Now I know that some leaders' time is literally out of their control because they don't run their own calendar. Their assistant or others on their support team schedule their video time, leaving little room for prep (typically not by choice—the leader's time is already booked up!). Whatever your role in this scenario, your best first move is to push for more prep time if you can.

Also, remember that you're not alone in this. Your director will work with you and your trusted team to help strategize the best communication style for your scenario. It's not just you and the blinking red camera light.

Let's take a closer look at your options. You can view the video examples mentioned here at vernoakley.com.

DIRECT-TO-CAMERA

As the name suggests, with this style the subject speaks directly into the camera. This format works especially well when you want to connect with employees or a specific group of people. Speaking straight into the lens is compelling because it gives the feeling that you're having a direct conversation with the viewers and looking directly into their eyes.

Often the most conversational approach is when the leader simply speaks without a teleprompter or interviewer to guide the conversation. The director can ask questions to prompt a topic or idea, but when the camera rolls, the leader flies solo. If your film crew shoots B-roll they'll stitch it together with your best speaking takes to create a short video that tells a powerful story.

A great example of this approach is Michele Scannavini's video introducing himself as the new CEO of Coty. We spent one hour filming Michele speaking into the camera. He had the freedom to try several takes until he felt totally comfortable with his message. We also spent a few more hours shooting B-roll of Michele driving his Vespa and interacting with colleagues around the office. These interactions showed Michele's warmth and creative energy—qualities that the Coty team was excited to see in their new leader. After filming, we condensed several hours' worth of footage into a seven-minute video that made a personal, intimate connection with viewers.

Speaking directly into the camera is not for everyone, but those who do feel comfortable with this approach tend to use it often. Scannavini says, "I found that looking directly at the camera was a better way for me to organize my thoughts and the message I wanted to deliver in the way that I wanted to deliver it."[1]

Even without B-roll, the direct-to-camera approach offers lots of room to show your passion as a leader and connect with your audience. Former Allergan CEO Paul Bisaro offers a great example in his brand refresh video. Although the entire video featured Paul speaking directly into the camera, it was still lively and impactful. This is because Paul, his team, and I worked through the material—in advance as well as on set—to make sure the message and delivery genuinely reflected Paul as a leader. We shot nine takes, each time working with Paul to deliver his key messages, refining the next take to emphasize a new point, or working on ending with power and a warm smile. His message was not only about the words, but also about his passionate and heartfelt delivery. You could literally feel his energy coming through the lens. Back in my studio, my crew and I turned forty-five minutes of footage into a three-minute video combining Paul's best takes.

Some busy leaders don't prep at all and simply read from a teleprompter on film day. It seems like an efficient choice since they can just show up, read the words, and carry on to their next meeting. In theory this is true, but most people—leaders and viewers alike—aren't happy with the experience. The truth is that a great teleprompter performance can take as much time as some other communication formats.

Most communication professionals and leaders I've worked with dislike teleprompters because they limit any sense of spontaneity and tend to make leaders look stiff on camera. Nevertheless, in certain situations teleprompters may be required. I discuss teleprompters thoroughly in the next chapter.

The one-way mirror is another tool for direct-to-camera performances, but unlike the teleprompter, it usually sparks a personal delivery that makes viewers feel you're speaking directly to them. The way it works is that a one-way mirror is placed in front of the camera. Then a beam splitter is used to project the director's live image onto the side of the mirror that the speaker can see. With this setup, the speaker can look straight into the director's eyes while talking, even if the director is standing off to the side. Meanwhile, the camera films through the glass as if nothing were standing between it and the speaker. One of the first one-way mirror systems, called the Interrotron, was created by director Errol Morris, but other filmmakers have created similar systems.

The Interrotron has been used to capture some unsettling performances. Errol Morris's searing *Fog of War* is a classic example. When former Secretary of Defense Robert Strange McNamara looks straight into the camera lens (seeing Errol's face on the mirror surface) and compares himself to a war criminal for helping to plan the horrendous fire bombings of Japanese cities during WWII, you start looking for exit signs in the movie theatre.[2]

DIRECT-TO-INTERVIEWER

In the direct-to-interviewer style, viewers are aware that you're having a conversation with someone else. That person can be on or off camera, but the bottom line is that viewers know you're not talking directly to them. While not as personal as direct-to-camera, this approach can still spark a powerful connection with your audience as they hear your message and witness your passion as you speak to someone else.

The same elements of time and preparation discussed previously apply here. Your director will help you refine your message and will shoot several takes until your delivery is clear and genuine. In post-production, your film team will edit a long interview down to a few powerful minutes and weave in B-roll if applicable.

People are perhaps most familiar with the **on-camera interview** since it's used in shows like *60 Minutes* and *Charlie Rose*. In this format, the interviewer and interviewee both appear on camera and viewers observe their conversation. While you're used to seeing this style on TV, remember that your video will be shot under much different circumstances. Unlike many TV interviews, the conversation in your video is under your control. Your interviewer won't try to get you to dish about topics you don't want to cover, or throw any surprise questions at you. You are in a safe space that you can trust. The goal is to help you communicate the message you want to share in what is an organic conversation.

Another direct-to-interviewer style is the **off-camera interview**. This is a kind of one-way conversation between the director, acting as the interviewer, and the interviewee. Viewers don't see the director because he or she is never filmed, and the questions are edited out of the final video.

When filming in this style, I try to create a relaxed, natural environment. If the person is seated, I sit across from them off-camera and close by the side of the camera lens. If they are standing, so am I, to keep the eye line natural. The person we're interviewing is not looking directly into the lens but rather at me. Because I'm so close to the camera, the eye line is such that the viewer feels he's in the room. Think of the camera in this case as the viewer's point of view.

This approach allows for a back and forth "conversation" and the kind of freedom I need to make a personal connection with the leader that helps them speak from the heart. This is the sacred space. I don't have to worry about camera angles or sound while in the moment. The crew is handling that. All I need to do is concentrate on helping the leader express his or her humanity and passion for the issue or topic at hand. It could be a merger announcement, a thank you to employees for a job well done, or a chance for a CEO to lay out his or her vision to employees.

The possibilities for this style are limitless. My team combined off-camera interviews with powerful B-roll to tell the story of how Tyco's ADT security systems helped protect the Magna Carta at St. Albans Cathedral in the UK. The format let us interview many of the project's leaders who wouldn't have felt at ease speaking directly into the camera. For the speaker, it's much easier to look at *me* than into a *lens*. This allows people to do what comes naturally. They are *talking to someone* and there just *happens* to be a camera rolling. The relaxed storytelling and B-roll combo made for a final video that told an epic story.

Spanx founder Sara Blakely offers an incredibly warm off-camera interview in a video highlighting her business tips for entrepreneurs.[3] The one-on-one dynamic makes for such a personal delivery it feels as if Blakely is sharing her success secrets only with you.

The **roundtable discussion** is a variation on the direct-to-interviewer style, but in this case several people are discussing a topic, sharing insights, and encouraging comments, and we see all of them on camera.

Since more than one person is being filmed, roundtables require multiple cameras. Footage from all of the cameras is edited together into a short video that captures the discussion's key moments and ideas.

The roundtable is particularly effective for discussing complex issues when you want different points of view to come forward. You may not want one person to be the total focus because someone in the group may contribute interesting and less familiar points of view to the audience.

This was the case when leaders from pharmaceutical company Allergan (then Actavis) filmed a roundtable. The talk showed Paul Bisaro, CEO of Allergan, and Brent Saunders, CEO of Forest Laboratories, alongside three other colleagues, discussing the companies' merger. At the time, Paul's role was shifting from CEO to executive chair while Brent would become CEO of the newly formed company. The roundtable was an excellent format for showing the camaraderie that existed between these leaders. Their non-verbals reflected their warmth toward one another, and emphasized that they were a strong, cohesive team with a shared purpose.

Paul said, "The five of us free-flowed conversation. . . . It was open, it was honest, it wasn't scripted. It was people talking genuinely from their heart and it resonated extremely well with the company."[4]

The roundtable creates the feeling of a team working together and shows how the team responds, reacts, and interacts with one another. It lets viewers see the speakers' passion and insider perspectives as they follow up with one another and build on a point in the conversation. The organic conversation creates a rich dynamic where people's ideas are sparked by what the previous speaker has said.

In most cases, someone guided by the off-camera director starts off the conversation. Everyone knows the subject of the conversation and the key points that need to be discussed, but it's important to keep it loose. You don't want to be so specific about the talking points that people start rehearsing what they'll say beforehand. That's a deathblow to the spontaneity and authenticity that makes this format so special.

My job as the director is to keep the group's energy up and move through the agreed-upon series of topics. Some people are good at succinct statements, and others drift off into long stories that are interesting but probably won't make the cut for a short film. If the conversation loses its focus, the director may call "cut" to refocus the discussion. I always make it clear that no one should ever feel bad about this call or become self-conscious about the amount of time they take to contribute.

The director in this scenario has to have a light touch. Before filming, I work closely with the leaders and/or their trusted team to create a list of topics that need to be covered. When the camera rolls, I need to make sure we've hit each point and that the communications team feels the same. I often consult with the leader's advisors as we're filming to ask if they think anything is missing. Sometimes, if something hasn't been brought up, I'll slip a question on paper to one of the panelists who are *not* being filmed at the moment. Once I'm out of the shot, I'll cue that participant with a hand signal to ask the question when the opportunity seems right. It's a continual team effort, especially when several people are on camera.

The only instance I'll ever have to stop a roundtable session is because we're changing camera cards, which in turn allows for a thoughtful break every twelve or twenty minutes. People can stand up and stretch, go to the bathroom, and recharge before the next take.

DIRECT-TO-AUDIENCE

I often turn to direct-to-audience video communications when the leaders I'm filming are camera shy but great in front of a room. In this setup, viewers see the leader speaking to a live audience. The actual scenario can range from a large public event, such as a town hall meeting, to a closed studio session with a small audience that we've cast just for this video. Using a small audience can create an intimate setting that allows the speaker to interact with others on camera in a way that plays to their strengths. The fluid format can also be beneficial to those who have little time to prep, since most leaders are already comfortable talking to a roomful of people. Now they just need to do it while a camera rolls.

I recently filmed three leaders at the consulting group KPMG. I joined the team just after they'd recorded a series of unsuccessful videos with another film crew. They felt they didn't come across authentically in those videos, and they wanted my help being real on camera. I knew I had to bring a fresh approach, but the leaders' schedules were airtight. They couldn't dedicate more than a couple of hours total to video prep, and their personalities were not coming through on a teleprompter. When I asked their advisors what these leaders were like, they told me they were fabulous in front of a room. Their hope was to capture the warmth, passion, and charisma that these guys radiated when talking face-to-face with their employees. But until that point, those qualities had been totally absent when the camera rolled.

I decided that if these leaders were great in front of a room, then that's where viewers should see them. We created an environment that looked like a TV show, with a studio audience, visible cameras on set, and a TV crew. My team and I carefully cast the "audience members," all of whom were KPMG employees. The people selected were passionate about the company and brought a great energy to the room, which made for excellent, organic interactions with the leaders.

The final video captured the leaders in their element: talking about their work with colleagues, answering questions, and discussing topics that viewers were eager to hear about. A lot of prep time went into setting up the "show," but all the leaders had to do was know the points they wanted to discuss, and show up ready for a great conversation. Our concentrated efforts on this one shoot yielded six short videos on a variety of topics. The company was armed with a small library of content that showed their leaders being real with their tribe, and speaking passionately about their shared work.

Direct-to-audience is a great antidote for the leader who is reluctant to speak to the camera at all. Years ago, I worked with an energy company whose CEO refused to be filmed. He felt he wouldn't be effective on camera. I always thought it would be important to get him on video, and I finally got my chance when he called a town hall meeting after a natural disaster. Without hesitation, this guy got in front of hundreds of people who had lost their homes and talked passionately about how his company would help the community. He said he would make a donation and give employees time off to help with relief efforts. Back in my studio, I edited segments of the CEO's talk into a larger video about the company. It helped give the company a face, and let the public know that the company's commitment to the community was coming from the very top. The CEO hadn't even realized the talk was being recorded, but when he saw the video, he conceded he wasn't so bad on camera after all.

In the same vein, this format is perfect for condensing a recorded speech into a short video. Editing lets us pull highlights from the talk and perhaps even pair that footage with B-roll for a short but powerful film.

GETTING TO THE TRUTH

Finding your sweet spot with an on-camera communication style is a big deal. But once you find your best format, it's still important to make sure you're personal and honest. A large part of my work is getting the leader to personalize their message. Let's say Ian Johnson is talking about his engineering department. He could say, "The engineering department has a lot of technical challenges to overcome in order to reach our goal on time. This will require meticulous attention to specifications, costs, and schedule."

But Ian would make a much better connection with the engineers watching the video by putting *them* in the picture, with something like, "I started out as an engineer and learned firsthand what demanding work goes on in the lab. Quite frankly I was just an OK engineer. But my experience taught me how to spot brilliant, dedicated engineers—and we hired them. I'm excited. There's a lot of hurdles to overcome on this project, but I know these men and women have the right stuff to get it done on schedule."

This kind of response is more from the heart. He's giving some of himself, revealing some new information about his past, and showing some vulnerability by admitting he might not be God's gift to the engineering world.

I find I get the best performance from someone if I've spent quality time with her or him before filming. Experienced communication professionals understand this, so they will try to arrange a short time with leaders before the shoot. During these meetings I don't usually discuss the questions I'm planning to ask in the interview. I've discovered that when I do this, they often try to write answers to these questions in advance and then memorize them for the camera. Not a good approach. Instead I ask them to tell me some stories about themselves—anecdotes and stories about their background, how they got into the business, their vision for the future—always hoping to discover what they really care about. I need to observe their natural communication style as they're speaking to establish what I am striving to capture on set. Later during the interview I may bring up some of the stories I heard earlier, and comment, "Hey Ian, didn't you tell me you were once an engineer?" Bingo. The CEO remembers our talk and gives me a great to-camera bite that helps establish his or her humanity.

I also observe the inflection and tone of voice and body language. Recently, a CEO on camera said he was excited about a merger. The words were right, but the energy, believability, heart, and passion that I saw during our earlier meeting weren't there. I paused the shoot for a moment and stepped out from behind the monitor. Then I looked him in the eye, one human to another, and asked him if he was really excited about this business move. "Jeez, Vern, of course I'm excited!" he said. His eyes lit up as he continued, his voice rising with excitement, "This is great for our company. Actually it's going to be really great for both companies!" I responded, "So glad to hear you express your passion. Now let's say it like that on camera." What a difference take two was. His excitement was 100 percent genuine and came through in his voice and body language. Even though his words weren't substantially different, his overall communication had completely changed.

The pre-film meeting is also a great time to get clear with your director about what you want to accomplish. Understand that this is different from telling your director what you want to say. It's more important to get clear on what you want your outcome to be. Do you want your employees to be inspired? Excited? Calmed? It's important to communicate your desired outcome so your director can help you get there. This is because every viewer listens from the seat they're sitting in. Whether your listener is a writer, director, accountant, or marketer, each person will have a different idea about what you're saying. And it's my job as the director to make sure you achieve your desired outcome with everyone on the receiving end. I do that by focusing on a passionate delivery and simplifying the message. The sacred space is critical here, as the director and leader tap into their shared trust to create an honest performance.

LOCATION. LOCATION. LOCATION.

Often leaders' schedules are so crammed I'm forced to take whatever I can get in terms of time and space. This can mean filming them in some generic conference room. Sometimes we get lucky. Perhaps there's a quiet outdoor courtyard, a lab, a private atrium, a state-of-the-art classroom, or some other location that feels right for the project.

Time permitting, picking a shooting location in which a leader is most comfortable can pay big dividends. The location can also frame the leader as a man or woman who might move in next door. Corporate communication expert Tina Orlando leveraged the power of location when she needed to introduce a new CEO to shareholders.

"We really wanted to convey a 360-degree sense of this person as opposed to some guy in a suit sitting behind a desk," Tina explained. "We actually spent a day at home with him and his family. And we shot him going for a jog, having a cup of tea with his wife and his kids, having breakfast, and petting the dog. And then the interview took place in different rooms in the house or in the garden, and people responded to it really well because they saw this individual, this sort of titan of industry as a regular guy that they could relate to."[5]

Not only did the interview take place in a comfortable location where the CEO came off like a new neighbor, but being in his house also provided the chance to film quick B-roll shots that humanized him.

Earlier, I mentioned filming a CEO on his Vespa. We've shot leaders visiting art galleries, walking through Grand Central Station on their daily commute, strolling the streets of Paris, touring shops to see their products on store shelves in Rome, and visiting a charitable school in Africa that their company funded. Seeing you on location helps to humanize you and connects viewers to your mission, your passion, and your story. It helps write the larger story of who you are—in moving pictures.

Find Your Groove in Front of the Lens—Key Ideas

▶ It's worth your time to think through the options for delivering your on-camera message. You may find that you're uncomfortable in one format but a complete natural in a different style.

▶ Once you find your best communication style, make sure your message is personal and honest. Remember that viewers want a story, not stats, and they want to get to know you as a person.

▶ It's best to shoot your film in a location where you feel the most comfortable, whether that's in your office, outside, in your home, or a mix of your favorite spots.

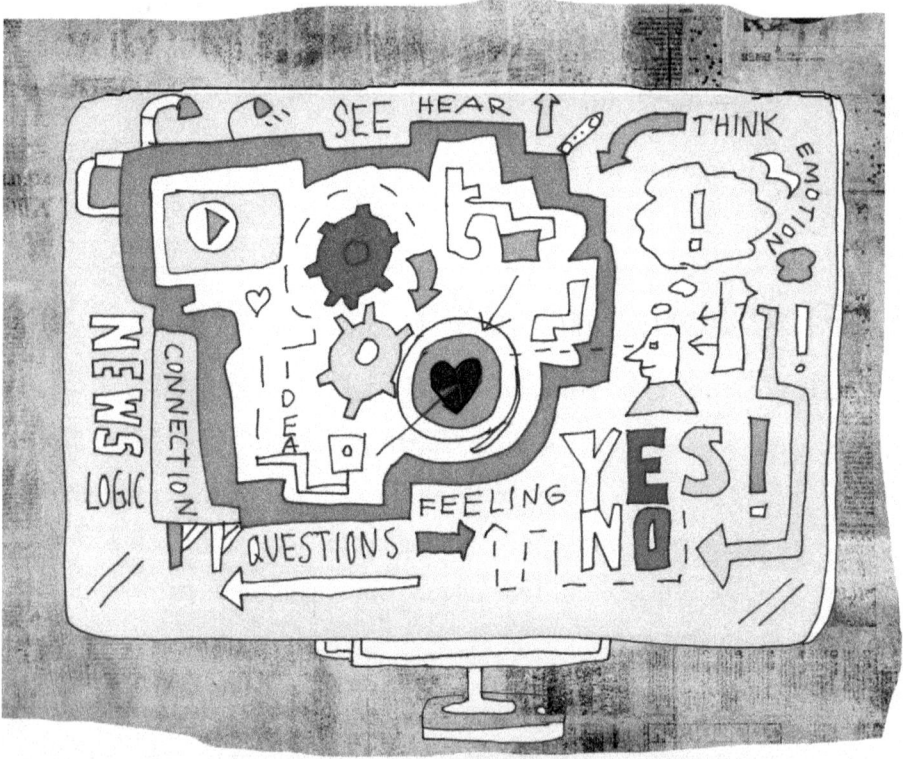

Anatomy of an Effective Video

Now that you're familiar with the core video styles, let's take a close look at a complete video in action. Satya Nadella demonstrated the power of finding one's groove on camera when he made his first on-camera appearance as Microsoft's new CEO. He opted to introduce himself via a walk-and-talk video interview—and it was very effective.

Nadella was interviewed by Microsoft's resident storyteller, Steve Clayton. The video runs just under five minutes. The interview is almost entirely done on the move, one seamless tracking shot of the two men walking and talking their way through Microsoft headquarters.

I think the choice of walking and talking was effective in part because it is as close as the CEO could get to an *in-person* talk with each employee. Clayton served as an employee proxy. Face-to-face communication is the most effective means of communication, but given Microsoft's highly dispersed audience, the best they could do was re-create that experience on video. It worked.

Nadella maintained the face-to-face intimacy. Never once did the CEO look at the cameraman who was walking backward the whole time. Instead he remained totally focused on Clayton.

Nadella is one of the most confident new CEOs I've seen on video.[1] The first question from Clayton was, "Who is Satya Nadella?"

Nadella answered,

> I'm forty-six years old. I've been at Microsoft for twenty-two of those forty-six years. I've been married for twenty-two years to a wife I've known since high school. We have three kids. Like anyone else with my experience, how I think has all been shaped by my life experience. And the one thing I would say that defines me is I love to learn. I get excited about new things. I buy more books than I read [laughs] or finish. I sign up for more online courses than I can actually finish, but the thing about being able to watch people do great things, learn new concepts, is something that truly excites me.

Nadella's delivery is not perfect. He trips over a word or three, but that only makes him more human. His body language is totally natural, and the content of his first answer is exactly what his employees wanted to hear first and foremost: who he is.

Nadella quickly shed some key information about his private life such as where he met his wife, how many children they are raising, and how long they have been married. At the same time, he says with some pride that he has worked at Microsoft since he was twenty-four years old. This CEO was a real person with kids, like many in the audience of his generation. By saying that he started working there in his twenties he also formed a link with the younger staffers at Microsoft.

By saying he bought more books than he could read and took more online courses than he could complete, he showed some vulnerability. He was a guy who sometimes bit off a little more than he could chew. But the reason he did? He was absolutely crazy about learning things. He gets excited by new concepts and watching people do great things. In just 1,200 words, Nadella managed to say, "I'm a human just like you. I love my wife and kids, I love working here, and I'm really excited about being CEO at Microsoft because I can watch people like you do great things!"

Embedded in his answers was a broad stroke. When you become boss, people want to know your expectations, and Nadella complied. He told them he wasn't asking for *good* things; he wanted people at Microsoft to do *great* things.

A lot was riding on this video, in particular because it represented Nadella's first impression to the public as the new CEO. Making a strong first impression lays the foundation for strong leadership, but ultimately respect will be earned by proving your authenticity through consistent actions that address employees' needs and your organization's objectives. Nadella's ease and confidence on camera set him up for a solid start—he made it clear that he believed in his people and that they could believe in him. Now all he had to do was get to work.

Ultimately, the only way to find your groove on camera is to test a few approaches (ideally well *before* filming!) until you feel comfortable. Here are a few key points to keep in mind as you work on finding your sweet spot. No matter what format you choose, your authenticity as a leader will shine through when your performance embodies most, if not all, of these elements.

CHOOSE YOUR BEST MODE

Work with an outside director or your trusted advisors if you are planning your first video as a new leader. Carefully consider and choose a communication style you are most comfortable with. This could be an off-camera interview, where the interviewer is not seen and the questions are not heard. Afterward, your comments can be edited together with B-roll to tell your story. If you're comfortable with the on-camera interview, you can use the opportunity to re-create a face-to-face experience for viewers, as Satya Nadella did.

MAKE NICE

Give a warm greeting. Depending on the format you choose, viewers may expect you to make good eye contact through the camera. Stakeholders are used to hearing warm and sincere greetings from political leaders, talk show hosts, and news anchors on television. They'll expect some warmth from you as well.

SHOW PRESENCE AND UTILIZE BODY LANGUAGE

Your workforce will respect you as a leader if you show confidence on video. Lean in every so often. Don't be afraid to move naturally, shifting your weight, pausing to look at the camera or viewer when appropriate. Discuss what you plan to wear with your director beforehand. What's appropriate garb for stockholders may not be the same threads you should have on to address employees. Do you need to wear a tie when you are sending out a holiday greeting? Let the makeup person do his or her job, and that means they'll pay some attention to your hair. Make sure you are comfortable with the way you look. You want to be you, not someone you think you should be.

BE SURE TO LISTEN

If you are in a back and forth on-camera interview or taking questions during a webinar, show you are a good listener. Everyone, especially employees, needs to know that their leaders take their opinions and points of view seriously and are fully engaged listeners. Ramp up your mindfulness. Be in the moment and listen.

DISPLAY ACCESSIBILITY

You can demonstrate you are accessible by the mode of communication you choose. A roundtable can serve to display that you are open to others' ideas. An on-camera interview can show your warmth as you interact with your interviewer. You can also use your on-camera appearance to mention how you can be reached, and that when you are contacted, you will listen carefully.

USE HUMOR

High-performance organizations staffed by dedicated, hard-working employees can be stressful environments. And while stress can be a good motivator to do great work, a little humor from the boss can take the edge off and go a long way to making work fun again. As a leader, remember, you set the tone.

SHOW VULNERABILITY

As I have pointed out earlier, showing vulnerability does not equate to showing weakness. Consider sharing some trial or personal story that relates to a pivotal moment in your career. Vulnerability can be a powerful and effective driver of employee engagement because it lets viewers see that they're working for a warm-blooded human who is not afraid to show his or her faults.

ADDRESS THE ELEPHANT IN THE ROOM

Often a new leader is hired because there has been a sea change. Sometimes these changes can mean layoffs for hundreds or even thousands of employees. Perhaps a merger is in the air or there's a rumor of one. Whatever the case, you would be wise to get a briefing from your CCO as to what your people are concerned about before you create your video. Ignoring issues of concern can be interpreted as arrogance or, worse still, a disinterest in the welfare of your people.

TELL THE TRUTH

A true leader never lies. Shape your communication to be pragmatic and honest. A merger, for instance, is a financial transaction that could benefit shareholders. If the leader says it's good for everybody, many know that it is not necessarily true for them. Some people may lose their jobs, and those who remain will face new bosses and changes in the system. The more you acknowledge the hard truths, the more appreciative your audience will be.

REINFORCE THE OBJECTIVE

If you are introducing yourself for the first time, is that really your only objective? Sure, people need to know who you are and what excites you. But if they know a big change is coming, they will want some reassurances that you are fully aware of its implications. You can also use this first meet and greet to bring up a specific project or change you want to implement. But in all of the above, keep it simple.

DISPEL WONKINESS

Some leaders pepper their addresses with "inside baseball" talk. Avoid this as much as possible. Don't mistake the use of convoluted operational terms and acronyms as a way to show people you "get it." All you will end up showing them is that you are not trying to connect as a fellow human being.

HOW NADELLA STACKS UP

Let's use the Satya Nadella interview as a case study and see how he stacks up. Does his performance embody all these elements listed above? Let me stress that his performance was not perfect, but in many ways it's in the "great" department. Based on the reactions of employees afterward, he did pretty damn well.

As of this writing, Nadella is getting good press. A year after taking the helm at Microsoft, stock was up double digits after languishing for years. According to one source, "Nadella has breathed new life into a moribund company that had lost its way under CEO Steve Ballmer. Nadella is thoughtful, serious, and seeks cooperation rather than confrontation. And he's a listener. Ballmer lacked respect among his own employees as well as among his peers in Silicon Valley."[2]

Looking down our list of qualities that communicate authenticity, Nadella aced several items.

Choose Your Best Mode

He clearly chose the best video mode for the occasion. Nadella looked completely natural walking and talking with his interviewer. He was totally at ease.

Make Nice

Nadella showed warmth. He could have kept more distance from his interviewer, but he chose to stay close and friendly, and this served him well.

Show Presence and Utilize Body Language

Nadella is well groomed. He wears an elegant sport jacket over a black tucked-in tee shirt. His interviewer wore what looks like an outdoorsy zip-up fleece. To me, Nadella's outfit is saying, "Hey, I've got some programmer in me, I'm a little nerdy like my people, but this jacket shows I'm ready to meet the board and the media to represent you all in a dignified way." His body language is excellent. Nice hand gestures when he's making his points. He smiles when appropriate, and his face becomes more resolute on more serious points. When he is asked how he felt when he took the position, he replies, "Honored, humbled, excited. Those are the three words that come to mind." The smile is replaced by a more earnest and thoughtful expression.

Be Sure to Listen

Definitely. You can see this through Nadella's body language. He is totally engaged. As I mentioned earlier, the interviewer is really the stand-in for the audience. He is asking the questions viewers have in their own heads. Nadella's eye contact never strays, he's not looking down at his feet or up at the ceiling or gazing into space. He is there, in the present. As for inclusiveness he mentions on more than one occasion that he wants employees to have more fun at their work and more relevance. "I want every one of us to find more meaning at work. We spend far too much time at work for it not to have deep meaning." He uses words like *we* and *us*. He acknowledges everyone there is working long hours, tipping his hat to his workforce and including himself as one of them. He waits until the interviewer has completely finished his question even though you can see he knows what he wants to say seconds earlier. He's showing some respect not only for the man asking the questions but also to the audience.

Display Accessibility

His body language and genuine friendliness certainly give the impression he's accessible but he doesn't specifically indicate *how* one could reach him, nor is he asked about that by the interviewer. He doesn't attempt any humor but says he wants employees to gain a sense of fun at work.

Show Vulnerability

As I mentioned earlier he does admit to buying too many books and taking too many courses he hasn't time to complete.

Address the Elephant in the Room

There's no discussion of Microsoft's then poor performance, but he's quite clear there will be a greater push toward cloud-based services.

Reinforce the Objective

If his objective was to introduce himself as an engaged CEO with a vision for the future, I'd say he succeeded. "The world going forward is more of a software-powered world delivered in devices and services, and I think we have the best platform to change the world."

Dispel Wonkiness

He never uses a word you haven't heard before. His style is conversational.

The presentation as a whole is effective. But there are flaws. The biggest is a statement by Nadella about making it easier for his people to be more innovative. "First thing I want to do and focus on is [to] ruthlessly remove any obstacles that allow us to innovate." This is a confusing statement. He should have said, "First thing I want to do and focus on is to ruthlessly remove any obstacles that do not allow us to innovate."

⏸

Finding your groove on camera takes time, a lot of trial and error, and patience. Remember to cut yourself some slack as you're building confidence in this strange new world. Work with your director and colleagues to figure out a format that works best for your message, and then get ready to make some mistakes. If Satya Nadella, CEO of one of the world's biggest technology companies, can fumble on camera and still look great, there's hope for all of us. I can't stress this enough: The goal is not to be perfect; it's to show that you're a real, warm-blooded human who cares about the people and the work.

Anatomy of an Effective Video—Key Ideas

- ▶ Nadella's delivery is not perfect, but that only makes him more human. His body language is natural and he focuses on telling viewers who he really is.

- ▶ It's important to show you're a good listener. Everyone needs to know that their leaders take their opinions seriously and are fully engaged listeners.

- ▶ Allow yourself a period of trial and error as you figure out your best video communication style. Remember that your film crew is there to help you figure out your best mode.

10

Teleprompter 101

"I'm Ron Burgundy?"

—RON BURGUNDY

In the movie *Anchorman: The Legend of Ron Burgundy* someone in the newsroom accidently added a question mark at the end of the TV news anchor's sign off—and the dimwit played by Will Ferrell reads it on the air. Here's the scene:

INT. NEWS SET:

RON BURGUNDY
(reading off teleprompter)
Well that's going to do it for all of us here at
Channel 4 News. Stay classy, San Diego! I'm
Ron Burgundy?

INT. CHANNEL 4 CONTROL ROOM:

ED HARKIN, NEWS DIRECTOR
(*slamming his hand down on his desk*)
Damn it! Who typed a question mark in the
teleprompter? For the last time *anything* you
put on that prompter Burgundy *will* read![1]

Taking the news director's comment to heart, a saboteur takes Burgundy's *verbatim* teleprompter-disability a disastrous step further the next night by inserting a new closing line sure to end Ron's career.

INT. NEWS SET:

RON BURGUNDY
And I'm Ron Burgundy. Go f*** yourself,
San Diego!

As Will Ferrell's character knew full well, teleprompters are a mixed blessing. Technically, they're meant to help on-camera performances by allowing the speaker to read from a prepared script. Using monitors and one-way mirrors, teleprompters display the text on an eye line so the speaker can keep his or her head up rather than looking down at a written page. But often you're so busy reading the words— there's little room for you to be yourself in the process.

Even the most seasoned performers struggle with the teleprompter. Academy Award–winner J. K. Simmons is a great example. In 2015 he won the Oscar for best supporting actor in *Whiplash*. He gave a heart-rending, off-the-cuff acceptance speech that was dripping with conviction and passion.[2] The following year, when he introduced the best supporting actress nominees, his performance was not as heart-felt. The effort Simmons put into reading off the screen zapped the personality out of his performance. Simmons even told a red carpet reporter before entering the building, "I hope I don't screw up reading the teleprompter!"[3] This guy has decades of training and an Academy Award under his belt—and he still feared the teleprompter.

Teleprompters are anathema to actors, and when leaders use them, their communications people usually aren't happy with the results. One such person is Tina Orlando. "I don't think I've ever really achieved a decent performance using a teleprompter," says Orlando. "You have to be very, very accomplished, and very practiced and comfortable to make it work. Most CEOs aren't because they've never committed the time to doing it. You can always see that they're reading, which automatically reduces the impact of that presentation at least 50 percent. People see CEOs reading teleprompters and they think, 'talking puppet.'"[4]

Part of the problem is that we subconsciously lower the bar when someone is using the teleprompter. We expect a certain level of inauthenticity to creep in when someone is reading off the screen, because it is nearly impossible to speak naturally. When leaders and their communication team operate with this belief, they're suddenly willing to settle for "good enough." They're more likely to check off the box that the communication is done, but are they really communicating in the true sense of the word? Are they making an impression, moving people, connecting and engaging with them?

In many organizations, those in charge of communications favor the teleprompter for one simple reason: Using one seems easier, more time efficient. They sit down, write a statement, get all concerned parties to sign off on the contents, and bring in the teleprompter. I worked with one CEO who went along with this strategy but like Tina, was not a fan. After wrapping a teleprompter shoot with him one day, he told me, "Hey Vern, I just realized something. If I cut the video budget, I don't have to do any more of these!" He got a twinkle in his eye just thinking about cutting the video budget so he'd never have to be uncomfortable in front of a teleprompter again.

I can understand where he was coming from. Speaking using a teleprompter can be stressful, but even a little preparation will let you take a deep breath and relax.

There will be times when leaders will need to depend on a teleprompter—however unpopular they might be—if they have to deliver concise messages. Sometimes they are a fact of life—like paying taxes and going to the dentist—so this chapter is devoted to helping you find the best way to work with these devices while still being yourself on camera.

HELPFUL PROS

Teleprompter operators are specialists who use a computer and special software to control the text. The operator can program the font, letter size, text speed, and amount of text on the screen at any given time. They can also insert pauses, underline key words, make a series of words bold so they read as a single phrase, and arrange the number of words on a line to help the speaker's pace.

A good teleprompter operator has no need to see you on camera; in most cases they are somewhere in the back of the room—or in another room entirely. All they care about is how you sound through their earphones. They also provide an invaluable backup for the soundman or mixer if you are recording a message that will be edited and distributed later on.

The best teleprompter operators are tactful, patient characters. If you ask their opinion on the substance of your script, many operators can help smooth out lines to make them sound more in the style of the way you normally talk off camera. This comes in handy if the director is occupied dealing with other matters. The teleprompter software allows the operator to make almost instantaneous changes in your text, eliminating hard-to-pronounce words and tongue-twisting phrases.

Many teleprompter operators are so valued for their ability to help people speak at their best, they are hired over and over again by CEOs, television personalities, and politicians, no matter the location.

MAKING THE MOST OF A NECESSARY EVIL

The biggest problem with teleprompters is that they often impede leaders from being themselves on camera. They don't leave much room for your personality to come through when you're reading your exact script off a screen. This is especially the case when the leader doesn't spend time getting familiar with the script before filming. Many CEOs want to show up, read the words (which unfortunately they may be seeing for the first time), and call it a day. That approach doesn't help anyone—not the leader or the viewer. But teleprompters do have their place in filming video if paired with even a little preparation.

Nobody can walk onto a film set and rattle off a great teleprompter performance on the first try. Remember those deer-in-the-headlights actors presenting at the Academy Awards? Even revered performers struggle with the teleprompter, so you can't expect yourself to nail it on the first or second take. It takes patience and lots of self-forgiveness before you can truly find your groove reading from a screen.

Also think about the two most common ways leaders use the teleprompter and what will be most useful for your situation. Sometimes you'll be required to read your whole script word-for-word, but if that's not the case, it might work better to use it as a notepad to help sequence your ideas, jog your thinking, or remember facts and figures.

If you fall into a situation where you *have* to use a teleprompter for your entire on-camera presentation (perhaps your legal team requires you to word something exactly right, for example), give yourself a break. Be aware that like any skill, you have to put in some real time to learn the craft. Most CEOs tell me that after a half dozen sessions, they start feeling more comfortable. And after a dozen, they have found their own rhythm.

Corp comm expert Jon Pepper points out that the purpose of these presentations "are more along the lines of bulletins or major announcements where you have to be very sure that you get particular wording or particular phrasing in a certain order where lawyers or financial disclosure is involved. You can't risk saying the wrong thing so a teleprompter is required."[5]

Just remember that if you lean on the teleprompter as a crutch, you'll need more time to find your rhythm in front of the lens. If you're forced to read from the teleprompter, it's still critical that you internalize your message so you can truly own it. That means understanding the key points, phrases, and words, and deciding how much weight to put on each one.

Also, take heart: Even if you're going to be the only person that viewers see in your video, the wonders of film can help make the process easier for you. For starters, since this isn't a live speech or broadcast, your director can work with you trying multiple takes until your message is convincing.

I'll talk more about post-production magic in the next chapter. If you're reading from a teleprompter, it's critical that you take the time to practice and internalize your message. That scrolling text will only hurt you if you rely on it completely. No amount of editing can make a stiff performance lively and powerful.

Here are some other key points to keep in mind when using the teleprompter.

Spend Some Quality Time Going Over Your Message with Someone You Trust to Give You Honest Feedback

You can get a lot done in a matter of minutes. Does the writing style of the message resemble the way you talk naturally? Practice out loud. Aside from building your confidence, it is a great way to find and remove tongue twisters. Sometimes just shifting two clauses around or adding a listener-friendly term can make your message more conversational. If legal is involved, make it clear they need to help you craft a message that sounds like it was written by a human. If your task is to deliver some bad news to people, show some empathy. It costs you nothing and builds your image as a good leader.

Have a Hard Copy of Your Message on Hand during Your Performance

Ideally you'd review the printed script before filming and mark important points you'd like to emphasize. If you don't do this in advance, it should be the first thing you do when you arrive on set. Work with your director and your trusted team to underline key points, massage words so they're in your voice, and cut unnecessary info. Your teleprompter operator can quickly update the text on-screen. And highlighting key points on paper first will help you remember to emphasize certain ideas when the camera rolls.

Meet Your Teleprompter Operator before the Shoot

Let the operator know he or she is important and you trust them to help you get through the shoot in one piece. A little humility goes a long way with any member of the film crew, but the teleprompter operator is your lifeline.

Add In Some Time to Rehearse on the Teleprompter

Reading from a screen will feel unnatural, so it's worth taking at least a few minutes to warm up before filming. You can also use this time to make sure the font and the size of the letters are easy to read.

DURING A TELEPROMPTER SHOOT

Remember: Leaders Lead and Operators Follow

Teleprompter operators *never* set the pace of your message—you do. You have more control than you may think. It's important to understand that the teleprompter operator is the cart and *you* are the horse. Their job is to follow along at your pace. Often people think the teleprompter is arbitrarily rolling and they need to keep up with it. They don't realize the operator is moving at the pace set by the speaker.

Vary Your Pace and Volume

By following some simple steps, you can sound less like a machine and more like a human. Alter your volume now and then, sometimes louder, sometimes softer. Aside from pausing to breathe, you can also pause at the end of important phrases to give your viewers time to ingest your thoughts. Vary the pace of your message to emphasize key points or set a mood. You might consider a slower read if you are sharing facts and figures. Again, remember the teleprompter is following you and not the other way around. A good operator will expect variation of pace, tone, emphasis, and will compensate.

Keep Your Eyes Still

Keeping your eyes still while reading is an acquired skill, but you and your director can easily *minimize* the perception that you're a reading robot by using a few simple tricks. I move the teleprompter far away from the speaker so his or her eyes don't need to move when reading the screen. I also put fewer words on each line, with larger text, so they can easily read the faraway screen without squinting.

On your end, try to move your head and use your hands (in moderation) to emphasize your points. Shift your weight from one leg to the other. If your body is moving, your eye movements will not be as noticeable.

Avoid the Blame Game at All Costs

Good teleprompter operators are not hurting for work. Like any other professional, they'll take only so much guff.

Ultimately, the biggest keys to mastering the teleprompter are patience and forgiveness. Understand that it's a tool, and like any tool, it takes work before you can master it. The teleprompter is not an easy way out of having to prep. I'd argue that it takes even more work to communicate authentically using a teleprompter than with any other communication format because it puts you in such an unnatural position.

Allergan executive chairman Paul Bisaro's teleprompter work got much better after he learned to trust the process and give it time. "I was very rigid when I started. Then I got the flow of it and I realized I didn't actually have to say every word and that I could take a breath and I could do a few things," he said. "As I settled down and decided not to worry so much about getting every word precise but to get some feeling into the message, I think I got better at it. But it took time. It took a lot of time. I'd say years, actually."[6]

Give yourself a break. If you're putting in the work to get better, know that's all you can do, and trust that you will improve with effort.

Teleprompter 101—Key Ideas

▶ Build a good relationship with your teleprompter operator. They are skilled and can often help you smooth out lines in your script, if you're forced to read from a teleprompter verbatim.

▶ It's important to prepare for your appearance even if you're using a teleprompter. Take the time to go over your ideas and what you plan to say. Do your best to internalize the content so you're not simply reading words from a screen.

▶ Give yourself a break if you can't get comfortable with a teleprompter. If you have the option of using a different communication style, try that. If you're forced to use the teleprompter, remember that it will take time and practice before you get comfortable using it. You can do it.

PART III

BEYOND THE LENS

11

Post-Production Magic

You already know you're not alone when it comes to making a great video. Your trusted team will work with your film crew to make filming as painless as possible. But the magic continues long after the cameras are put away. Video's flexibility lets us leverage a wealth of post-production tactics that will turn hours of footage into a powerful final piece.

Technology lets us do some amazing things, but the bottom line is that we edit each video around your best moments. We start by scouring the footage for a few magic seconds when your words, vocal intonation, facial expressions, and body language come together to create a real, truthful statement. It's those seconds when your eyes light up as you're talking about an exciting new project. Perhaps you're leaning forward, speaking in an excited tone that shows your passion for your subject. When we find such spots, we mark those clips and then cut the remaining footage around your best shots to paint the larger picture.

If we can show a leader's humanity for a few seconds throughout the video, that energy will color the entire piece. Viewers will see the larger picture through that same lens of empathy and passion. The key is to begin and end the video with your best moments. It's important to start strong, and like in gymnastics, ending solidly is also critical because it leaves viewers with the sense that you're a poised and confident leader.

When I'm directing, I keep a mental image of the sliding bar at the bottom of a YouTube screen. It helps me make sure I have a clean opener and ending with enough pauses for editing throughout. It's a way for me to keep the editing process in mind as I'm shooting and collecting the raw footage. If the speaker stumbles, I can slide the bar back to zero and have them do another take, or skip back a few seconds to have them repeat a small section. Then I work with our film editor to select the best takes, which he or she will later cut into the final video.

Here's a closer look at the strategies we use to make your video soar. The more you know about the process, the less intimidating it becomes and the more you can concentrate on being the best and most authentic you.

THE EDIT ROOM

During the shoot, the director has your back. After the footage is delivered to the editor, it's his or her role to make sure the director *and* you look great. Typically the editor views the unedited footage and whittles it down to the strongest material. Today, almost all professional editing is done using nonlinear edit systems. The footage is uploaded onto a central, high-capacity hard drive linked to a high-speed computer chock-full of state-of-the-art editing software. In most cases, the editor views the "camera original" or raw footage on one monitor and the edited footage on another. Using a mouse, he or she can select any part of a scene down to the frame and move that scene or clip anywhere along the timeline of the film. The editor can use the audio that accompanies a specific shot and manipulate or move that audio elsewhere. Music, either composed specifically for the project or taken from a music library, is layered in with the camera audio and video. Sound effects can also be laid down and adjusted.

Editors bring a fresh eye to every film. A good editor will often discover an angle on a project no one during the planning stages or shoot ever considered. They might hear a phrase from a leader that was recorded by accident while a light was being adjusted and find a fresh perspective no one imagined. Ultimately, the editor is crafting the story that was shot on location. And when you watch a great editor's work, you walk away with the feeling that the film could only have been put together precisely in the way it was.

"Drama is life with all the dull bits cut out."[1]

—ALFRED HITCHCOCK

I have worked with many talented editors who have cut some of my company's most successful projects. They frequently work under heavy time constraints, sometimes editing as much as four hours of footage into a two- to five-minute film under a tight deadline.

To get to the core of a film quickly, our editors will often look for the strongest, most germane pieces of your performance and string them together. This is what we call a radio edit. We're literally taking the footage, ignoring the picture, and stitching together the pieces to tell a story. It doesn't matter if there are jump cuts (when the picture suddenly skips to a slightly different position due to the cut piece of dialogue) or if the visuals are out of focus. All that matters is that we've put together a coherent story. From there, we have many techniques for editing the video footage to smooth it all out and make it visually compelling.

THE POWER OF B-ROLL

We've talked a lot about B-roll already, but I want to highlight its power to help your film team edit raw footage into a short video. To be clear, not every video will have—or need—B-roll, and that's fine. It's not right for every project, but when we do use it, it opens the door to endless creative editing options.

B-roll can work as glue when we cut up lengthy material into smaller statements by eliminating whole phrases and joining the first snippet to the last. For example,

> I started out as an engineer and ~~learned firsthand what~~
> ~~demanding work goes on at the lab.~~ Quite frankly I was
> just an OK engineer.

The gist of what's been said retains its basic meaning; the line is just shorter and less detailed. Editors can also smooth out language by electronically deleting stumbles and "ums." Audio editing software makes it possible to construct a single word from syllables of other words. The editor can also borrow one word from an entirely different statement and insert that word into another sentence. This process of hacking up and recombining of words is nicknamed "Frankenbiting." Frankenbiting was coined by "reality" TV producers who use editing software to make people *say* things they really *didn't* say. We use the process to allow you to say what you *wanted* to say but somehow flubbed.

Once the audio is finalized, we can use B-roll to fill the gaps. You see Ian on camera as he says he started out as an engineer. The editor cuts out the chunk that says "learned firsthand what demanding work goes on at the lab." To avoid a jump cut, the film cuts to an entirely different shot that's related to the sentence while we continue to hear the subject's voice. He keeps talking, but the picture over the talk is a B-roll shot.

In this case a B-roll shot could be as simple as seeing Ian walking into the engineering building. We then have the option of cutting back to Ian seamlessly where he finishes his statement (no viewer would remember what position his head was in last time we saw him on camera).

When used well, B-roll tells its own secondary story line that deepens the main message with strong visuals. Seeing Ian walk into the engineering department is a film editor's visual Band-Aid. The shot takes care of the jump cut but it does nothing to enhance Ian's humanity. But what if Ian walks into the building and meets some guys he's worked with for years? They shake hands and smile at each other and they are not faking it. Through their body language we can see that

Ian's colleagues like and respect him and vice versa. The B-roll is telling its own little story—Ian's a real guy who enjoys strong relationships with his colleagues. He's worth listening to.

There are also times when a leader's actions in B-roll footage express the culture of the company. Remember that video I mentioned previously by the CEO of Coty, Michele Scannavini? The beauty and fragrance company's motto at the time was Faster, Further, Freer. Michele often rode his Vespa to work in Paris. "It makes me feel free," he told me. When I asked Michele if we could film him on his Vespa for B-roll he immediately saw the connection to his company's brand.

"The famous Vespa shot, which has become an icon for myself and for the company, was a very interesting way of expressing the culture of the company. It's not so much that it was fancy or nice to see me going around on a Vespa, but it was a way to express the company's Faster, Further, Freer motto and make it iconic."[2]

EDITING WITHOUT B-ROLL

B-roll isn't the be-all, end-all of film editing. There are other strategies to avoid jump cuts, like using graphics to stitch together various takes. Pretty much anything goes here—from maps or quotes to baby pictures. When done well, graphics can add as much texture to the main story line as B-roll can. The nonprofit Code.org used graphics to great effect when filming YouTube CEO Susan Wojcicki. In the video, Wojcicki tells the story of taking her first computer class in college. As her story unfolds, the video cuts to a photo of young Wojcicki wearing her college hoodie, years away from her rise at Google, and later, YouTube. While this particular video does have B-roll, its use of graphics adds more depth than the B-roll. We see photos of Wojcicki during her early years at Google, screen shots of some of Google's early home pages, even a photo of the Google hockey team. Altogether, the graphics bring Wojcicki's brief story to life while offering a behind-the-scenes look at a beloved company. The video is definitely more than the sum of its parts.[3]

There's also some amazing technology available that lets editors seamlessly cut and merge content without relying on B-roll or dealing with awkward jump cuts. My favorite among these is morph technology, which allows us to edit a speaker without cutting away from his or her face. The morphing technology merges several visual frames into a series of facial muscular movements that look natural when done well. If the editing quality is subpar, it will look like the speaker has a slight tic in his or her face. Morphing technology also cleans up any gaps in the footage, and when done well, looks seamless. You can see an example of this, and the other videos mentioned in this chapter, at vernoakley.com.

Tactful camera work can also go a long way in editing. The art lies in capturing the words and broader communication by varying both the angles and framing (such as close-up, medium, and wide shots). But it's important to match the right strategy to the right context. For example, if the speaker isn't using a teleprompter, I'll shoot using multiple cameras. Having multiple camera angles offers room to create an organic flow in the leader's words. This allows us to create a seamless, short video with visual variety rather than a long, single take. This was the case with an executive I filmed who was introducing herself to employees after joining the company. She was reluctant to go on camera, but she loved giving speeches and speaking spontaneously from the heart. We wanted to catch her in her element, so we filmed about thirty minutes of unscripted footage. Her natural, passionate delivery let us use editing to emphasize certain points. We could go to a close-up when she was making an articulate, passionate point, or a wide shot when she was speaking more broadly and gesturing with her hands. She was the only person on-screen, but multiple camera angles helped us condense a half hour of footage into just a few minutes.

I don't feel it's necessary to have multiple cameras when working with a teleprompter because it's usually obvious that the speaker is reading from a screen. In this scenario, it doesn't look natural to cut to a different camera angle, but we can still edit by varying between close-up, medium, and wide shots.

When editing teleprompter footage, we want to try to get a coherent performance from beginning to end based on many different takes. We also look for the moments when the leader stops using the teleprompter as a crutch and speaks from the heart. We'll even focus on a little eyebrow raise or grin to show some personality. The goal is to insert the humanity by stitching together the best parts of each take.

STRIKE UP THE BAND

Music plays a big role in our projects. In almost every case, as soon as our editors rough out a radio cut they'll start building the music track since it's integral to the film's mood. Let's say you have some exciting news to share with employees or stockholders. The right music can signal and build that mood of excitement and good news. A good music track can allow you to be authentically you by providing an emotional underpinning to your words. Music can evoke urgency, gravitas, caution, hope, and empathy.

APPROVAL

As soon as the radio cut is fleshed out with music, sound effects, and narration (if needed), the project is now close to the total running time called for. The next step is to show it to the client for approval. If we've done our homework, the leader and his or her trusted team may only ask for a few tweaks. The project then goes into a finer finishing phase where the picture is color corrected and the sound tracks are fully mixed.

Post-Production Magic—Key Ideas

▶ Post-production video tactics like B-roll, music, and editing help create a rich, moving film. But remember that they don't get you off the hook from having to prepare for your on-camera performances.

▶ If your video doesn't include B-roll, editors can still seamlessly cut and merge content without awkward jump cuts.

▶ If you prepared but still worry that your presentation isn't great, remember that just about anything can be fixed with editing. You have plenty of freedom to stumble as long as you give your video team enough original footage to work with.

12

The Rewards of Preparation

"In theory there is no difference between
theory and practice. In practice there is."

—YOGI BERRA

Not everyone is intimidated by the thought of appearing on video. Many leaders have no problem with it—they're happy, even excited, to share their thoughts as the camera rolls. But no matter where you fall on the stage-fright spectrum, your performance will benefit from practice and preparation. If you feel you're already great on camera, your confidence could be a blind spot for areas that need improvement. And if you're all jitters, you likely need to put in more practice.

This chapter is full of fascinating examples of intense practice and preparation. I'm not advocating that you take your efforts to these Herculean levels right now. But I *do* think it's a good idea to explore how truly great leaders and performers practice and prepare. Their stories are inspirational and can help us assess our own performances. I've also included some more down-to-earth stories of preparation taken from my own experience working with high-performing clients, media experts, and fellow directors. This chapter is not about being perfect (no chapter in this book is!). It's about the rewards of being prepared before going on camera.

The truth is, *not* being prepared for a video appearance isn't really an option. There's too much at stake when your communication is recorded. When you're having an off day at the office, you can offer an in-person explanation on the spot—maybe you're jet lagged, sick, or recovering from a bender at the class reunion. If you're not expressing yourself well at a meeting, you can stumble around your ideas until your colleagues finally understand what you've been trying to say. They'll most likely forgive and forget a few imprecise communications that take place in the privacy of your office, but your viewers won't be as understanding if you're inarticulate on camera. A poorly planned or fumbled message tends to stick in people's minds more than a decent one does—for a number of reasons.

If colleagues or employees within your organization see a poor video, they will feel embarrassment by association. They may worry that you're making the whole company look inept. Other viewers may feel that you have not only wasted *their* time but also squandered valuable organizational resources. They will assume you had adequate time to prepare your message and that you hired a professional crew to film it—and yet you didn't bother to work on delivering a well-crafted message. If you are a leader, you are always expecting the best use of resources from your people. Suddenly it will look as if you are doing the opposite. What message does that send?

Also remember that video lasts indefinitely. A poorly executed meeting or a clumsy conversation will eventually be forgotten, but your video communication will forever live on the Internet, or your company's intranet. Anyone can pull it up at any time and see your poor performance.

Some leaders go ahead with important announcements completely unprepared. I think that's a big mistake and so does Bernd Beetz. Beetz has served in c-level positions at several international beauty and fashion companies over the years. He didn't reach his level of success by shooting his videos from the hip. Recently, Beetz told me that making the personal commitment to getting the message right was a crucial part of his video communications. "If you get yourself on film, you're locked down. People can always pull up the film and say, 'Look, on that occasion you said this, on that occasion you said that.' You have to be prepared to commit yourself on a piece of film. I think that's the biggest hurdle for people to get over."[1]

Your company is counting on you to do your due diligence and prepare. Many top leaders in the private sector might participate in a dozen or more videos a year. But how many hours have they devoted to thinking through the material they want to cover or practicing *how* they would present their message to their viewers? How many hours? Frequently, not a whole lot.

OK. Now think of how many hours you've practiced your golf swing or tennis backhand. I'm guessing many, and you practice them seriously, perhaps working with a coach or a pro.

"There is in the act of preparation, the moment you start caring. Only then are you ready to speak to an audience. Because they will listen only when you care what you speak about."

—WINSTON CHURCHILL

PREPARATION IS A TWO-WAY STREET

I've said it before, but it's worth repeating: You're not alone in this. Just as you'd work with a coach or other expert to improve your piano or tennis skills, you have a support system in place to help enhance your video performance. It's important to note that there are several types of preparation for an on-camera appearance, and each person on your team will help in different ways. For example, your communications team will likely work with you on messaging. Your director will help strengthen your performance and streamline the words that your support staff put together for you. Executives often show up on set with a lengthy script that can't possibly fit within a short video. It's great that they've spent time prepping the message—but it usually needs to be condensed. A great director will help distill a pages-long script into a few short, powerful words by zeroing in on the most important points. He or she can also humanize the message by helping you turn those facts and figures into a story. The sacred space offers a safe environment where you can work with your director to get comfortable with your material. And as the director, part of my job in maintaining the sacred space is to know the material as well as the leader does.

Becton Dickinson CEO Vince Forlenza realizes that a director who has done his or her homework has a profound influence on his own performance. "If the director is well prepared, it makes it so much easier for me," Vince said. "Because then the director is asking the right questions and has done enough work to have a real sense of what's important and what's not. It becomes much more conversational between the two of us. If I have to direct you to ask the right questions, then I have a whole other role in this thing."

CEOs and their trusted team are often at odds when it comes to allocating time for preparation and practice. If you are on the communications side of the table, heed Vince's lament: "What drives me crazy, Vern, is when people ask me to do something and then they don't give me time to prepare."[2]

This point is true in business, and it's true in the movies. It reminds me of an anecdote that a director friend shared with me. He had asked an esteemed actor to play a small role in a new film. Knowing how busy the actor was, the director promised that it wouldn't take more than two days of his time. Filming would be easy and efficient. The actor refused the part, explaining that although filming would be quick, he'd still need to devote at least two weeks to preparing for the performance. He'd need time to get to know the character, his lines, and how the role fit within the film's larger story. That couldn't happen overnight—and he didn't have two weeks to spare. My director friend knew the guy was right. He didn't continue pressing him to take the job.

Now, perhaps you're not in line for a feature film, but the point still applies. Your final video may only be two to three minutes long, and filming might take a day, but you can't expect yourself to put on a great performance without some level of practice and preparation before film day. Even the most talented speakers among us need time to absorb the message and make it their own.

Leaders also need to consider their colleagues' side of the equation. If advisors are not given the time to help the boss prepare, and his video is a flop, they are often blamed. Even if you can't dedicate hours to preparation, a few thoughtful minutes can make a difference for all involved.

Try making this investment: Sit down with your communications team for a few minutes and lay out a plan on how best to allocate prep time for a video appearance. Why? You may have projected such disinterest or dislike of video they don't dare bring the subject up. Make it clear you want to improve your performance and you want them to have the time to discuss the content and how best to prepare your delivery. These talks can happen in deliberate meetings, or they can be woven into the fabric of your interactions with your trusted team. Even a small amount of prep time can go a long way. Some communications professionals have told me that they sneak in planning conversations with leaders over coffee, or in the few moments before a different meeting comes to order.

> "It usually takes me more than three weeks to prepare a good impromptu speech."
>
> **—MARK TWAIN**

WHAT GREAT PREPARATION LOOKS LIKE

I have found that when my clients take my advice and put time into practicing and preparing for the camera, something bordering on the magical happens. Because they have learned and absorbed all the points they want to make on camera, they can redirect their energy toward delivering that information from the heart. Like a solo violinist, they can move with the music and become one with the spirit of the piece, rather than being stuck turning pages on a music stand while they play.

After you craft a message, your job has just begun. It's worth taking the time to practice your delivery until the message becomes a part of you. That's when your humanity will begin to shine through—when you stop trying to remember what to say, or how to say it, and simply communicate in your own natural style. Winston Churchill read all his addresses out loud before he faced a camera or a live audience. He eliminated fancy words and tongue twisters, and inserted dashes to remind himself where he would breathe in between words. He knew his content and the meaning behind each phrase. Whether he realized it or not, by staying true to his own natural speaking rhythm and eliminating words he might have stumbled over, "The British Bulldog" was managing and maintaining his own authenticity.

Paul Bisaro offers another great example of smart preparation. Paul knew his on-camera appearances needed help, but he was spread so thin that he thought he'd only ever have time for quick video shoots using the teleprompter. Filming had turned into such a bad experience for him that he admitted he was more comfortable running a mega corporation than doing a video shoot. "I feel very self-conscious and uncomfortable most of the time," he told me. Much of his video work involved standing before a teleprompter reading some technical announcement. Furthermore, the appearances were sporadic, which didn't help matters.

Paul knew that in this age the currency of communication for leaders is video and social media. He was also keenly aware that teleprompter appearances can't deliver the kind of passion and inspiration he wanted to impart to the people in his organization.

"Your employees and colleagues have to feel that you care and that you're enthusiastic and you're trying to pass on the enthusiasm to them," Paul said. "If you can convince them of that, then you'll get people to all pull in the right directions. You don't get everybody and not everything's perfect, but it's a big step in the right direction. The problem is most CEOs don't have the time to sit around and think about stuff. There are people walking in your office 24/7 or you're getting calls."[3]

Like all CEOs, every second of Paul's day was accounted for. He didn't like teleprompters because he felt he came off as stiff and wooden, so he knew he had to change his approach. As a leader who shows up to work at his multibillion-dollar company driving a pickup truck, Paul had a lot of personality to share and he knew the teleprompter wasn't letting his true qualities come through. But where would he find the time?

By working together, we discovered that the best alternative was the direct-to-camera interview. As director per that mode of shooting, I would not be seen and my questions to Paul would not be heard. I stood behind the camera and Paul looked at me as he spoke, giving the appearance that he was looking directly at the viewer.

Our approach offered a chance for Paul to be himself on camera by simply answering some casual questions. He spoke candidly about topics that were near and dear to him: the company brand, his passion for the new company name, and his perspective on the exciting changes ahead. We set up three cameras at different angles so we could edit Paul's multiple takes together without using B-roll. His delivery was so personal that it could stand alone. We cut his answers in such a way that he was telling a story to his audience. When viewers watched the video on their laptop or in a company town hall it felt as if he were talking to each person one-on-one. You can view the video, and the others mentioned in this chapter, at tribepictures.com/leadershipinfocus.

We managed to accomplish all of this utilizing the same amount of time Paul would set aside for a teleprompter shoot. While Paul couldn't give me much of his own time, he made sure I had enough time to prepare questions with his trusted CCO Charles Mayr. Charlie identified the key points we needed to hit, and I fashioned a list of questions for Paul that would get us to the answers in the most natural way possible. Paul would set some of his time aside for prep and some last-minute consulting with his CCO.

"I would prep by going through the prepared materials and then spend fifteen to twenty minutes thinking about the concepts I wanted to articulate. I would also spend a lot of time talking to Charlie about messaging and what he thinks the company needs me to address."[4]

This prep time helped Paul to be more relaxed on video and I think he even began to enjoy our sessions. In the slim forty-five minutes he could give us from his totally booked day, we were recording material that would take other crews a lot longer to accumulate.

No doubt, you're beyond busy, but it's worth taking the time to prep, even if it's just to figure out the best way *to* prep! In Paul's case, he figured out that with a little help from his team, he'd only have to put in a few minutes of his own time to completely transform his performances. If he hadn't done this, he'd still be dreading those teleprompter sessions, and putting out ineffective videos in the process.

> "In every branch of art, the work of preparation, ruled by discipline, should finally disappear, so the elegance and freshness of the form should strike us as spontaneous."
>
> —PABLO CASALS

PLAY BACK SOME PROS

If I'm lucky enough to break bread with clients, I like to play them some video samples of leaders who communicate well. I stress to my clients that the point of the exercise is not to mimic these communicators but rather to get a feel for various styles and strongpoints they might experiment with. Some of these taped leaders use humor and timing, others remain unflustered when they stumble on a word, and still others have learned to keep excellent eye contact with their interviewer.

Everyone from great actors to championship athletes checks their performance in video playbacks. Consider asking your communications team to assemble you a half hour of CEO-MVP clips. Viewing them together could trigger a great and constructive discussion from both sides of the table. Try to isolate spots in your on-camera appearances where your personality shows through and where you are being the best you on camera. These will help guide your performance in future projects. You might also take a look at some leaders who went the extra mile.

The late Steve Jobs was one of the most outstanding presenters of our time. He spent days on end rehearsing important announcements and presentations. He required the same of outside speakers at Apple as well.[5] They had to practice at length or they were shown the door.

Even before Apple exploded into a global giant, Jobs found his voice and style. His simple black shirt and blue jeans seemed to take the focus off *him* and place it on the *message*.

His messages were straightforward and simple. And they were a heady and sophisticated blend of sales pitch, gizmo presentation, and corporate hutzpah with overtones of an evangelical preacher thrown in for good measure. These videos and live presentations were the products of *weeks* of work for scores of communications people, not to mention Jobs himself.[6] But for Jobs, much of his preparation and practice came down to the human-to-human delivery.

If you enjoy playing back the pros, you may be inspired to push yourself beyond basic practice. Astrophysicist Neil deGrasse Tyson, director of the Hayden Planetarium in New York City, has done just that. Tyson is well known as an astrophysicist who can connect on camera to convey scientific complexity with a sense of humor. In an interview with Dave Davies of *Fresh Air*, Tyson explained his well-known "gift" for talking on film is all about preparation. For example, when he was determined to make his first appearance on *The Daily Show* a success, Tyson studied how Jon Stewart talked to his guests.

"I timed how long he lets you speak before he comes in with some kind of wisecrack or a joke. And what's the average time interval of that? Is it a minute, ninety seconds, thirty seconds? I would create a rhythm in the parceling of the information I would deliver to him so that a complete thought would come out. . . . No, it's not a gift. I work at it."[7]

Tyson is quick to point out that his "gift" is not a gift at all. It's simply the result of preparation and practice—two primary forces in the cosmos of effective communication.

The Rewards of Preparation— Key Ideas

▶ Take the time to prepare before a video shoot. Remember that a poorly planned video presentation can stick in people's minds more than a good one.

▶ If you can't dedicate hours to preparation, find a trusted person on your team to work with your director to figure out the best approach for your video. You'll still need to set aside at least fifteen to twenty minutes to think about what you want to say, but your colleague can help work out the details of a strategy with your director.

▶ Part of your director's job in maintaining the sacred space is to know your material as well as you do.

▶ A great way to prepare is to watch other leaders on video. What approaches do they use? What can you learn from them? Also watch your own performances to see what you might like to change.

13

Making the Leap from Being Good to Great on Camera

By this point you know what it takes to pull off a solid video appearance. We've explored the importance of speaking from the heart, of being authentic, and of being true to your own values. I made the point that it's OK to reveal some vulnerability on camera because it shows your human side to the viewer. Those instructions were designed to get you to "good." Getting to "great" builds on these qualities but moves into the higher dimension of *performance*. This is not the same as acting, but we can borrow some skills actors use to become great on camera.

I compare the difference between being good and being great on camera to my experience of learning how to ski. All I wanted was to make it down the hill without breaking a leg. It took me five lessons just to make it down the hill intact. That's where we are in this book:

If you have applied the on-camera techniques I've laid out, taken the concept of authenticity to heart, and learned to prepare and practice, you are well on your way to being good on camera.

I want to acknowledge that being good on camera is all you may ever need or want to do. You will already stand a head or two higher than most leaders you'll see on company websites or YouTube. You have acquired a fundamental understanding of the value of a good director and film crew and how they can help you advance your vision and leadership. You have seen how a modicum of preparation can go a long way to presenting the best you on camera. You have reached the bottom of the beginner hill standing on both skis.

What I mean by becoming "great" is graduating beyond the bunny slope and being able to enjoy a weekend skiing with friends. You're no longer trembling at the top of the beginner's hill. You're comfortable with your environment (one that was once foreign and terrifying), and you're confident in your ability to glide down the intermediate slope. It took several lessons and even more hours to reach this point, but now that you're here, it feels effortless and even fun.

The leaders who never sharpen their on-camera skills beyond the beginner's hill will be just fine. They'll make solid videos that communicate their message and they'll carry on with their day. But to truly enjoy the rewards of a memorable ski weekend—to create videos that touch lives and rouse action—you'll need to put extra time into those lessons, and even more into practice. But it will be worth the trouble once you experience the view from the top of that hill.

The truth is, you don't have to do anything different from what we've been discussing to become great on camera. It's just a matter of doing a lot more, and understanding what a lot more looks and feels like. Yes, I mean more practice and prep, but also taking the time to think more deeply about your message, how you're connecting with your audience, and how you can best prepare for every video shoot.

BORROWING FROM ACTING TO GET TO GREAT

To get to great, it's important to first understand *performance*, which is not the same as acting. Acting involves taking on the characteristics of a different person. Actors study how the other person speaks, how they move, how they communicate, and then embody that person's traits. Kevin Spacey describes acting this way in a promo video for his MasterClass workshop: "The craft of acting is to step into someone else's shoes, someone else's ideas; to look at something in a mirror and not see ourselves and not feel weird, but feel free."[1] I love this explanation of the art form, and it can help us understand what we're *not* doing when we're performing. Performing is not embodying someone else—it's capturing the elements of *your best self* on a good day. In fact, to borrow from Kevin, I'd say performing is to look in the mirror and *see ourselves*, and not feel weird, but free.

Despite their differences, we can borrow from acting practices to help you put on a great performance. While it may sound simple enough to just *be yourself*, the reality is that you have many sides, and you'll need to channel the right version of you that's appropriate for each situation and each audience. This doesn't mean you're being a phony. You're simply showing the side of yourself that fits the context. Imagine how a TV executive might dress and behave when pitching a new idea to his board. Now picture that same person out at a theater festival scouting new actors. Or imagine a chef who is meeting potential restaurant investors in the afternoon, then spending the night training his kitchen staff. Each person would dress and carry him or herself differently in each context.

When performing on camera, showing a certain side of yourself is a lot like playing a character in a film—only it's you every time. This is where actors' techniques can help with your performance. For one thing, actors always look for the truth in the parts they play. They spend an enormous amount of time rehearsing their lines and movements—not to make them fake, but to imbue them with humanity.

This technique harkens back to one of the first systems of acting, developed by Constantin Stanislavski in Russia between 1911 and 1938. Stanislavski's system required actors to summon up realistic emotions for the roles they played by harnessing memories of real experiences.[2] If a player had a scene where his character was deliriously happy, the actor would summon up a joyous memory from his real life in order to convey the emotion authentically. This is essentially the technique that actors like Meryl Streep, Al Pacino, and Paul Newman use to summon a real smile on camera. They give you pieces of their lives—the ultimate gift of an artist to the audience—and for our purpose, the ultimate gift a leader can give to their audience.

While your role on camera will change with each context, the need to show that you're a thoughtful, genuine human will be constant. Your task is to channel a part of your true self that's in tune with each message. A great way to do this is by sharing relevant stories from your past. Great leaders often use storytelling on video by framing a past event into a present context.

PepsiCo CEO Indra Nooyi had every viewer smiling when she shared the backstory of her first US job interview on Makers.com, a website dedicated to stories from great female leaders. She recounts that when she had just arrived from India to study at Yale, the only clothes she owned were saris and jeans. Neither would work for a job interview. So she hit the local Kmart to buy an interview outfit with all the money she had: fifty dollars. Indra was proud of her new polyester pantsuit, but she ran out of money for shoes. She ended up wearing big orange snow boots to the interview, and despite the ridiculous garb, she got the job. The CEO pairs this story with a discussion of her work ethic during her rise up the corporate ladder. "I've always focused on doing a damn good job, and just hoping the rest takes care of itself."[3] Hearing about the young, slightly clueless Indra elevates her video from good to great. By sharing the truth, she transforms herself from an untouchable CEO to a flawed, vulnerable (but still powerful) human to whom anyone can relate.

Indra's story is a good reminder of why many theater directors won't practice stage direction or movements until the actors have memorized their lines. They know a performance can't be authentic until the actor has internalized the message. Once you know the words, you can then add the meaning. You're a step ahead of actors since you already own your words, stories, and the information you plan to share. Like Indra's job interview flashback, your stories are a part of you. And if you're passionate about your message, that enthusiasm is also woven into the fabric of who you are today. Actors need to discover the playwright's meaning, or filter in their own meaning, before they can bring a role to life. You're already there, but your humanity won't come through unless you take the time to internalize your message. Imagine if someone other than Indra read her story from a script. It would lack heart and soul—the elements that made viewers truly connect with her.

Stanford Graduate School of Business professor Elizabeth Blankespoor validates this point in a paper she coauthored. The paper reveals that a company's value can actually be influenced by how well investors feel the CEO presents him or herself in front of an audience. Blankespoor points out that training is essential when CEOs make a public appearance. She explains, "It won't fool investors into seeing you as something you're not, and that should never be the goal. But it may bolster your confidence and help you relax, so your own true qualities shine through."[4] An article in *Insights by Stanford Business* further develops Blankespoor's point, saying, "Executives might take a cue from theater: Good actors don't 'put on' a character; they find it in themselves. So when you get up in front of that audience, know yourself, be yourself, and show them who's boss. That's what they've come to see."[5]

FROM MIND TO BODY

As Stanislavski continued to refine his system, it required that actors study external physical actions, gestures, verbal, and physical communication.[6] Laurence Olivier, the great stage and screen actor, favored the external approach. To become the Moorish General Othello, Olivier spent hours blackening his face to feel the part. Olivier used external mechanisms of makeup, costumes, facial expressions, and physical gestures to bring the *feeling* of a character inside himself. He then brought the constructed character back out of himself in front of the camera.

As I mentioned previously, actors in biopics study videos or old films of the real people they play every chance they get. By copying the contorted posture of Stephen Hawking, Eddie Redmayne not only looked the part, he felt it. To be great on camera you need to feel great in real life. Like Eddie Redmayne, you can use your body to inform your performance.

Review your past appearances on camera with trusted advisors. Compare the gestures and postures that projected your message from those that distracted from it. Were you speaking in an appropriate tone? Identify the moments where you felt comfortable and analyze why. What were you wearing that day? Did you feel good in that outfit or did you feel confined? Was the lighting too harsh? Was that why you were squinting? Keep a list of what made things feel right and what threw you off. Then refine the positives and make them yours.

PRACTICE TO BE GREAT

Earlier in our journey I made the point that being good on camera means "practice, practice, practice." Being great on camera requires a focused approach to practice, and part of your journey is figuring out a system that works best for you through trial and error. Your goal is to engage in the kind of practice that lets you explore, borrow, customize, and incorporate great communication techniques wherever you might find them. I've witnessed major comedians hone their skills early in their career using this approach. They'll write new material, perform it, see what got laughs and what flopped, tweak it, and try again. They'll do this in front of audiences of different sizes and demographics to analyze varied responses, all the while embracing the journey of improving their work.

Daniel Weiss used a similar approach of analyzing his performances so he could improve them. Daniel is a world-class art historian and an accomplished speaker on camera and off. I can attest to that fact, having worked with him when he was president of Lafayette College. Daniel's art background coupled with his business and communication skills have earned him a new post: He left academia to become president of the Metropolitan Museum of Art in New York City.

But Daniel wasn't always a star on camera—in fact, as he tells it, he wasn't even good when he started appearing in videos. Daniel has worked hard on mastering his on-camera skills, and that investment has helped earn him one of the most prestigious positions in the art world today. Daniel found his own way by confronting his limitations and letting them guide him to solutions. "I think the secret to my success as a public speaker and on camera is knowing my strengths and my weaknesses and using them."[7]

He started out thinking he was a natural on camera—until he saw and heard himself for the first time during a media training session. "I walked into that room with a great deal of self-confidence that I was good at this, and I was mortified by what I saw. I talked too fast. I walked around so much the camera couldn't keep pace with what I was saying. I was not a good public speaker, not as good as I thought I was. The first time I saw myself, it was a window into the ways in which I was deficient in this skill I thought I had."[8]

Like most effective leaders, Daniel Weiss is hard on himself, but sometimes you need that kind of oomph to get better. Just make sure you know when to tame your inner critic. Personally, when my inner critic starts talking to me in a way that I would never speak to anyone else, not even my worst enemy, it's time to give the critic the boot. A coach I've worked with suggested that I give my inner critic a persona so I could talk to it and make it go away. I've made my critic a villain with a handlebar moustache. Other times, he's a lizard. When he crosses a line, I feed the guy a grape and tell him to go away.

Part of Weiss's improvement process was analyzing his day-to-day personal style, how he best communicates with people, and then transposing that style to video. "The audience craves authenticity. Each person should try to find the mode of doing this sort of work that feels most comfortable for them, in which they are most natural. There is no one-standard approach that works for everybody. But it's important to have some sense of how you like to communicate, and then translate that to how you communicate with the camera."[9]

Daniel's process for overcoming obstacles to being effective on camera is a good model. First, he assessed his on-camera skills with a media professional and discovered, to his surprise, he wasn't that good. For one thing, his body language was out of control and not natural. This replay experience inspired him to analyze how he could be more authentic and more comfortable on camera.

Next, Daniel started to look for methods to reach his comfort level, which in turn would allow him to be more himself. One of his most important steps in this direction was finding his own way to structure *and* remember the content of his message. Dan told me that he became more comfortable when he created a loose structure for his ideas and how they might interplay as takeaways for his viewers. All that he had to do then was commit this structure to memory.

"What are the points that I want to make? How do they relate to each other, and what are the overall themes I want people to walk away with? I'll very often sit down with a piece of paper and write those points in the order in which I think they should be delivered. The act of writing them down is enough for me to remember them and then I don't have to remember anything."[10]

So once Daniel realized he was not a natural on camera, he managed to isolate the reasons why. He then raised his comfort level by coming up with his own system to organize his ideas—always keeping the audience takeaway in mind. Then he began analyzing *how* he would deliver his material in a way that felt natural. For him, that meant keeping his ideas conversational first and foremost.

"I'm always far more comfortable and effective without a script. It's enough for me to just know what the general topic is. If I'm following a script, then I'm engaged just in the process of *remembering* what I'm supposed to *remember*. My presentation is more wooden and rote than natural. But I'm good at extemporaneous speaking around themes that we've agreed we should cover. That works for me. I don't ever use a text, unless I have to."

Finally, like so many other effective leaders I've worked with, Daniel learned that often the real goal of an on-camera appearance is not so much to unpack a bunch of facts or concepts. It's more about using your authenticity to make an impression on viewers, first and foremost. If people are impressed by your passion for a topic, they'll find ways to read more about your vision on their own.

"The audience doesn't care at all that you cover everything you think you need to cover. They won't remember anyway. What they will remember is the way in which you communicate and the basic ideas and themes that you're expounding upon. So if you can touch them and move them with your general set of concerns and themes, then they'll remember that and they'll learn as much as they want to thereafter based on that inspiration. They're sure as hell not going to remember everything anyway, so I don't worry about that."[11]

I think this is great advice and it cuts to a major preconception many of us have when it's time to step in front of a camera. We can't talk about everything *all* the time or we lose the audience in the weeds. Often, people are watching your video to see what kind of person you are over and above what you have to say in the way of content. There is no standard approach that works for everybody. To that end, I'm not sharing Daniel's approach as a gold standard, but I do think it's a good example of a leader who came up with his own customized action plan: Find your weaknesses, analyze how to boost your confidence and comfort levels, and most importantly, remember your main objective is to connect with your audience above and beyond the content.

THE *GREAT* MIND-SET

Another important element of great on-camera performances is getting into the right mind-set. Just like practice, your journey to the right mind-set will be personal, and one that you'll most likely discover through trial and error. You have to figure out what works best for you. I have a pre-camera routine that gets me into the right mind-set for a video shoot, whether I'm directing or appearing on-screen. I wake up early to watch the sunrise and connect with the earth. Then I take some time to journal and exercise. If I'm directing, by that point I would have ideally had at least one prep session with the leader and/or his or her team, so I spend the rest of the morning reviewing the questions and key messages we discussed in our meeting. I remind myself of any common ground the speaker and I might share, whether we're from the same home state, have a mutual love of sports, have kids the same age, or love art. Whatever it is, I remind myself of the connective tissue that could bring us together quickly. If I'm appearing on camera, I try to imagine my best self answering questions about topics we'll be covering. I'll try on different emotions as I visualize giving my answers, aiming to be confident, friendly, warm, honest, caring, and empathetic. Then I get to the shoot early to maintain my calm.

Many leaders today turn to mindfulness, meditation, and visualization to get into the right mind-set. At their core, these techniques are all about setting time aside to clear your thoughts. This might seem woo-woo, but many successful leaders swear by these methods to help them get ahead. Volumes have been written on these practices, and it's beyond the scope of this book to discuss them in detail. But I will offer a brief overview on each technique because I believe they can be powerful tools for becoming great on camera.

Mindfulness

Mindfulness is just being aware. It can be practiced informally or with a teacher. According to proponent Elisha Goldstein, PhD, "When you're practicing it informally, that means that you're simply attempting to be more aware in everything that you do—and that mentality can be infused into pretty much anything. But the formal practice of mindfulness is mindfulness meditation."[12]

Mindfulness meditation is when you intentionally ascribe some time to pay total attention to being in the moment. It's being aware of the "now" of things, says Goldstein. "The goal is to learn to be really present, to the point that when you feel yourself reacting a certain way, you can step back and literally change your knee-jerk reaction so you do something in a different way."[13]

Mindfulness can be a great help to anyone performing on camera. If you are completely present and not thinking about your last meeting or the one coming up after the shoot, you're much less likely to make mistakes. If it's an interview, you will pay better attention to the questions from the interviewer and therefore give much better answers. If you stumble for whatever reason, you will not instantly worry about what people are thinking about you. Instead, you will simply realize, *I made a mistake, oh well*, and continue on.

Meditation

Physical stretching exercises can help you relax your body. Meditation is a way to stretch and relax your mind. According to some sources, spending as little as five minutes each day in meditation can deliver real benefits above and beyond feeling calmer on camera and off. Research indicates that the practice lowers your blood pressure, helps you sleep more soundly, and will bolster your immune system. Meditating will improve your mood, focus, mental clarity, and memory. Studies by world-renowned psychologist Michael Posner show that meditation will change the way your brain functions,[14] leading to the growth of new brain cells and neural connections.

Visualization

Visualization, or as some call it, "mental imagery," can have a positive impact on your performance. Take sports performance. Imagine running a perfect marathon or hitting a killer backhand playing tennis. The key is to imagine this in your mind over and over again with a positive outcome.

Medical chemist and PhD David Hamilton has written several books that fuse science, the mind, and spiritual wisdom. He also writes a regular blog for *The Huffington Post*. "Every thought alters brain chemistry," says Hamilton. "The same kind of thought repeated often actually shapes brain structure and has a chemical impact around the body." Hamilton cites a Harvard study where researchers had volunteers play piano notes each day for five consecutive days. They were compared to volunteers who imagined playing the notes. After the five days elapsed, there were marked brain changes in the brains of both groups. If you looked at MRIs of both groups, there was no way to distinguish one from the other.[15]

I know leaders who imagine themselves giving authentic, passionate, and persuasive performances on camera. When practicing jokes, they picture people laughing; when telling stories, they visualize the listener leaning in to absorb the tale. They even imagine being a viewer, hearing each point of the address. In my own experience, running through this mental imagery first is a great confidence builder. I can sense some change in my head.

You may never take up mindfulness, meditation, or visualization, and that's perfectly fine. You can still be great on camera without them. The goal is to figure out a system or routine that will get you in a calm, focused, and productive mind-set.

FAKE IT 'TIL YOU MAKE IT

We know our minds can change our bodies. Going from a walking pace to running requires us to first make that decision in our minds. Even if we jump out of the way of a falling piano, that involuntary impulse comes from the brain. But as I touched on earlier in the book, this brain-to-body messaging can go in reverse.

Remember that simple exercise I suggested that has to do with smiling? If you purposely smile, you feel better. The object of this simple exercise is to make the point that our bodies can change the way we feel and think, and applying this principle to communications can make us great on camera.

In her TED talk, Amy Cuddy makes the point that our bodies can change our minds in powerful ways. She pointed out that in primate hierarchies, alpha males have high amounts of the hormone testosterone (the dominance hormone) and low levels of cortisol (the stress hormone). The same holds true, it seems, for powerful and effective leaders.[16]

Cuddy took some volunteers into a lab and had them adopt what are called high-power poses. In one such pose nicknamed the "Wonder Woman" by the media, her subjects stood upright, feet apart, with their hands planted on their waists. After standing in this pose for two minutes, hormone samples from their saliva showed consistent and significant increases in testosterone and lower levels of cortisol.

In a carefully fashioned subsequent test, volunteers adopted high-power stances before going through a difficult job interview. Other volunteers were told to adopt low power stances such as making themselves small by sitting and clasping their arms around their bodies. No one knew how the poses figured into the interview—they just followed Cuddy's instructions. The job interviewers had no idea which volunteers did which exercise beforehand.

As it turned out, the people who were selected for jobs were those who took the Wonder Woman stance. They were still themselves, they weren't acting, and yet their power attracted their interviewers. Cuddy uses the old catch phrase, "fake it until you make it," to describe this phenomenon. While it's true that people assumed or faked the stance, it's equally true that when they went in for their interviews they were still their true authentic selves but they were a more powerful version of themselves.[17]

The moral of my story breaks into two parts. First, take some time to experiment with power poses. Try them before a presentation and see if people pay more attention to your message. You can even stand up and try one right now. Experience its effects on your body. Second, using your body to inform your mind and using your body to get down to your more powerful self are examples of the methods we can adopt to go from good to great on camera. This is about "performing" and not "acting." You are still you, but you are putting your absolute best foot forward—being the most powerful, persuasive you.

"Gratitude is the sign of a noble soul."

—AESOP

GETTING HELP FROM TRUSTED ADVISORS

If you've gotten this far in the book, I'm going to assume you put a lot of weight on the value of communications. I'm also going to assume you will take to heart my advice about getting good feedback from a trusted advisor. They keep their ears to the ground to inform you what people throughout your organization are talking about. They give you truthful appraisals of your performance on camera and conduct follow-ups on the effectiveness of your messages. If you're a CEO, you might find a trusted advisor in a great CCO. But no matter what your leadership level or the size of your organization, don't underestimate the value of a communications person at your right hand.

Recently, I attended a conference that featured the legendary Jack Welch, former CEO of General Electric who was named Manager of the Century by *Fortune* magazine. Welch stressed that you need a CCO who understands truth and trust. "CCOs and CEOs have a unique relationship. There's got to be total trust. The CCO's relationship with the CEO has got to be closer than with anyone else on the staff."[18]

Allergan executive chairman Paul Bisaro understands how important this relationship can be. He moved past being good and became great on camera by listening and trusting his head of communications, Charlie Mayr. Paul told me, "I was lucky to have Charlie. His skills in communicating or understanding how to communicate, not just to employees, can't be understated. And every CEO needs to know, they need to have somebody that they can rely on to help them do that. You can't do that yourself."[19]

If you don't have a CCO, a trusted communication coach can help you get to the next level. Nobody at the top of his or her game has reached that point without a coach or mentor. Tiger Woods is on his fifth swing coach since starting his career.[20] Even top executives who *do* have CCOs turn to trusted advisors to help them get to the next level. Angela Ahrendts, SVP of retail and online stores at Apple, credits each stage of her career, and each of her mentors, with teaching her something new: "left brain" skills from Warnaco ex-CEO Linda Wachner; the importance of getting the product right in a monogram business from Donna Karan; and managing a multibrand company, presenting to a board of directors, and talking to investors from Liz Claiborne chairman, Paul R. Charron.[21]

There will always be someone who can help you get better, whether they're already on your in-house team, a friend or colleague, or a hired coach. Find someone you trust, and open your mind to learning something new from him or her.

Ultimately, the difference between being good and being great is summed up by these words written by Marshall Goldsmith in his book *What Got You Here Won't Get You There*: "The only difference between us and the super-successful among us—the near-great and the great—is that *the great ones do this all the time*. It's automatic for them. For them there's no on–off switch for caring and empathy and showing respect. It's always on."[22]

Making the Leap from Being Good to Great on Camera—Key Ideas

▶ One of the simplest ways to get to great is by practicing. To be truly great, you will need to invest time in practicing and preparing for *all* communication projects.

▶ Consider Daniel Weiss's approach for customizing an action plan: Watch at least one of your on-camera appearances to determine what needs improvement. You can do this on your own or with a colleague who understands your communication goals. Analyze how to boost your confidence and comfort levels. Then work on each element step-by-step.

▶ Take a tip from great actors, who put a piece of themselves into each of their performances. They rehearse their lines and movements, not to make them fake, but to make them authentic and natural.

▶ Practice power poses before a presentation. They can result in a more confident you and a more engaged audience.

PART IV

VIDEO'S SURPRISE SUPER-POWERS

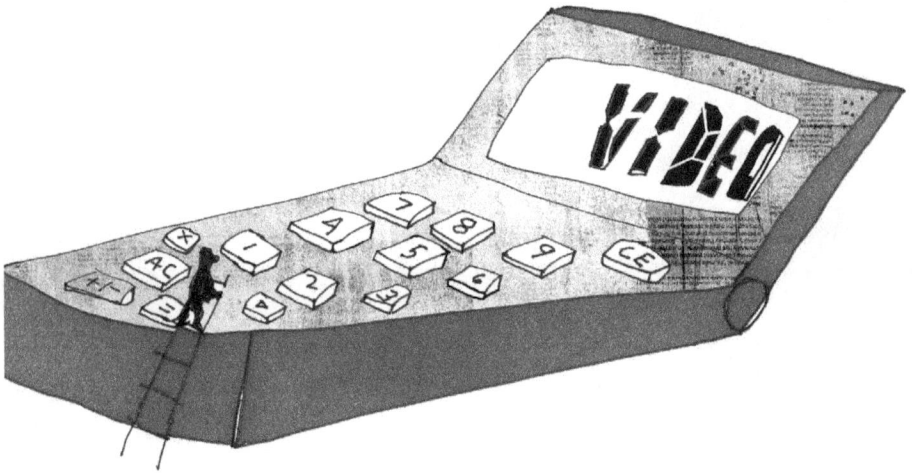

14

Return on Investment

Video communications are becoming ubiquitous in business. Leaders of all stripes—from bootstrapping entrepreneurs to CEOs of multibillion-dollar companies—are investing in video to forward their vision and inspire action. But how do they know whether their video budget is money well spent? Businesses often obsess over return-on-investment (ROI) metrics, and with good reason. It's important to know whether your endeavors are turning a profit. If they're not, it stands to reason that the project is not worth the investment.

The question of ROI is simple enough. Finding an answer is where things get tricky because ROI can't always be measured in a scientific way. It's a complex concept with multiple methodologies. And while it's easy to measure concrete results like click-through rates or sales, leadership communication is not about sparking a transaction.

It's about aligning your tribe with your vision, and inspiring them to become champions for your shared cause.

How do you measure whether your investment has accomplished *that*? No math equation or online metrics will give you the answer.

You're not making videos to sell widgets (unless you are), so it doesn't make sense to calculate ROI in terms of dollars out vs. dollars in. And frankly, with so many people claiming to be ROI experts and measuring it in different ways, you're best off to come up with your own way of measuring your success based on what you're trying to accomplish. Your likely goal is to make an emotional connection with your audience, show them who you are as a leader and a human, and inspire them to take action. With that in mind, your best measurement might be to observe people's actions in response to your videos, assess how they feel, and uncover what your company morale looks like.

Earlier in the book, I mentioned the famous WWII radio speech given by King George VI. It's a great example of heartfelt and real communication from a leader. The return on investment for the once-stuttering monarch was immeasurable. By stepping out of his comfort zone, he proved himself worthy of the crown and rallied the British people to the war against Hitler and the Nazis.

When John F. Kennedy invested in the power of film, he took a giant step toward the oval office. Following the advice of director Arthur Penn, Kennedy looked straight into the lens of the camera in the presidential debates with Richard Nixon. The strategy allowed JFK to project authenticity and confidence that Nixon simply could not match.[1] ROI? Kennedy became our thirty-fifth president.

Jumping ahead to the twenty-first century, video has enabled forward-thinking leaders like Elon Musk, Indra Nooyi, and Sara

Blakely to strengthen their organizations' cultures. More and more CEOs are going on camera to reach out to employees to foster a deeper meaning and purpose in the work they do week after week. This may not lead to immediate *dollars in*, but the long-term benefits of building employee relationships and morale are invaluable, and immeasurable.

RETURN ON INSPIRATION

Jack Welch, former head of General Electric, suggests that CEOs should think of themselves more as CMOs: Chief Meaning Officers. Along with inspiring their people, Welch believes that keeping people in the loop is an investment well worth the effort.

Part of the reason for any leader's existence is "to give purpose to their teams. To relentlessly, passionately explain, 'Here's where we're going. Here's why. Here's how we're going to get there. Here's how you fit in. And here's what's in it for you.'"[2]

I've made the case throughout this book that the most effective way to communicate your passion and vision as a leader is through on-camera appearances. Reaching out to viewers through a well-prepared and practiced video is the closest thing to a face-to-face conversation—the gold standard of human communication. Your message can be viewed online or through your organization's internal network or on a host of Internet platforms.

The benefits of effective communications are huge, but what kind of investment do companies put aside for it? Compared to other segments of the budget pie such as marketing, the average number of dollars set aside for communications is skimpy. For large companies, the average allocation for marketing ranges from 12 to 30 percent of total revenue. According to a poll compiled from eighteen large corporations, allocations for communications average 0.154 percent of total revenue.[3] But even these modest outlays bring in surprising returns.

In one study of employee communication, researchers from Towers Watson discovered that "companies that are highly effective at employee communication are 1.7 times as likely to be high-performing than companies that are not highly effective at communication."[4] And again regarding Jack Welch, when General Electric did a survey of employee attitudes they found out that "employees who are more satisfied with their supervisor's communication interactions are more likely to be as productive as they can be [and] less likely to be looking for a new job."[5] Not a bad ROI.

Container Store founder and CEO Kip Tindell has seen such a good return on communications, he's come to see it not only as a tool but as an essential act of leadership. "We believe in just relentlessly trying to communicate everything to every single employee at all times, and we're very open. We share everything. I always make it a point to give the same presentation I give at the board meeting to the staff, and then that trickles down to everybody in the company."[6]

Return on investment for great communications can take many forms. It can increase performance and the number of returning customers. Inclusive communications bring meaning and satisfaction to employees above and beyond their paychecks. Knowing their leaders care about them, are truthful, and invested in their futures keeps talented staff from walking out the door. Google Kip Tindell under the "video" category and you'll find a number of links, including one on the BigThink.com site where he makes it clear how much he values his employees. "We wind up with great people and they're very productive and they're very innovative. Then you can pay them well and you need to pay them well."[7] He adds that his employee turnover is in the single digits while most companies' are in the double digits. Big Think videos are available to the public, and you can bet Tindell's people are among the people watching. They absolutely know how their CEO feels about them and they stay. This makes the company stronger and saves money. Good ROI.

RETURN ON IMAGINATION

I've noticed that when companies reach out with imaginative messages, the return benefits can be incredibly powerful. I call this ROI the Return on Imagination. If your video can help people visualize what the future might look like, or visualize how your company, school, product, or initiative is going to influence and shape society, those images become pictures that people can embrace and then can begin to create. Your message quickly turns into *their* message. It says, "We're going there—together."

Not everyone sees the same picture you do, but video gives you the chance to literally bring your vision to life. Once others see it and understand it, the lightbulb goes off. It feels real. Forget the PowerPoint slides and think: If a picture is worth a thousand words, how about a moving picture with sound and multimedia? Its potential to rally others around your vision is limitless.

A while back, we did a sales piece for a major telecommunications company. It was edgy, shot in black-and-white, and the protagonist was a slam poet. The client's ROI was twofold. The contact person we worked with garnered some instant prestige with the company. He became the go-to guy whenever the company needed a compelling video presentation.

The other return was less expected. Even though its purpose was for marketing, the film became an inadvertent recruiting tool. One of the staff told me the film inspired him to apply for a position at the company. "Any company that's willing to do something that unusual, I felt, must have an amazing culture. And that's why I wanted to come here." The video essentially recast the image of an old communication company into a brand that was high-tech, useful, and a place where even millennials wanted to work. Video was the perfect medium to connect with a generation who grew up on visual media. This wasn't your grandfather's or even your father's company anymore. It was a place where young innovators were eager to bring their talent. They wanted to be a part of the change this company was making.

This isn't unusual. Often a video with one intended purpose ends up having other, unexpected uses. We see it happen with school admissions videos, where a short film aimed at recruiting students ends up attracting other professional talent as well. You can't anticipate—or track—that kind of ROI, but it's there.

Some videos unintentionally recruit talent—but others are made for that very purpose. We even see surprising returns on those projects. One of our most memorable recruitment films was made for KPMG. The video highlights the story of one employee who felt ready for a change, but struggled to see where he could go within the company. An in-house mentor worked with him to find a new position that would be a better match, and now that employee is thriving. I shared the video at a sales meeting with a prospective client as an example of our work. After the video finished, people in the room were saying, "Hey, I want to work for *that* company." The same thing happened at three other companies I visited.

These people were not saying, "I want to work for that company" to be funny. They were saying that there was something so appealing about the recruitment film that drew them in. The video was infused with the hiring company's values: They were caring, innovative, they worked for good clients, and they had high ethical standards. The people in the film conveyed these values with conviction. The fact that communications people from an entirely different company fantasized about leaving their jobs to join the other company was an awfully satisfying return for me personally. That kind of impact is also an example of how any effective, imaginative video yields unexpected returns.

CALCULATING THE FINANCIAL ROI

I get it—this is business. While the ideas of Return on Inspiration and Return on Imagination are intriguing, most companies still want to know whether their video budget is worth the cash leak. I can say this: Tribe's videos have helped raise more than eight billion dollars for universities and colleges. The cumulative production costs of those videos were under two million dollars. Were the videos worth it? Well, we can't isolate how much they were responsible for bringing in, because each video was part of a comprehensive campaign involving communications teams, websites, events, etc. But the videos were the emotional connection to the story at every turn. Each event kicked off with a video screening. They were played on iPads in donor living rooms. They were the first thing you saw when you visited the organization's website. Would the campaigns have been as successful without the videos to connect viewers to the organization's goals? I suppose that, technically, we'll never know, but market research can help point us to a solid answer—for my videos and for yours.

If you're determined to pull hard stats on your video's ROI, your first step is to figure out exactly what you want to measure. Communications strategist Molly Borchers polled some of the sharpest minds in her field for insights on measuring the ROI in PR, a similarly hard-to-track arena. Consultant Shonali Burke's advice is especially relevant to video. She says, "One of the most important questions to ask when trying to figure out how to measure the success (or failure) of your campaign or initiative is, 'Why?' Why are you investing time and resources into a particular campaign? What do you hope to get out of it?"[8]

Again, the answer to your "why" might be hard to calculate in dollars and cents, but if your video has, say, a marketing or fund-raising purpose, the metrics could be right in front of you. Crowdfunding offers a unique view into how investments in video can quickly bring in a cash return. Think about this: If you've ever funded a project on websites like Kickstarter or Indiegogo, what convinced you to make your pledge? Maybe you wanted whatever perks were being offered at your funding level, but before you even knew what those were, you likely watched the campaign's video. And if the video didn't move you, you were probably less likely to make a pledge—or else, not a very big one.

The experts at MWP Digital Media analyzed 7,196 Kickstarter projects to determine the advantages of including a video in your Kickstarter campaign. They discovered that projects that include a video are 85 percent more likely to achieve their funding goal. "The better quality and more convincing your video is, the more you will raise," MWP researchers concluded. "Consider it a vital investment in your dream."[9]

Even if you've never backed a crowdfunded project, it's worth taking the time to click through a few successful projects and their videos. You'll find that the people on-screen—from entrepreneurs to artists—embody many of the characteristics of a great on-camera performance discussed in this book. You can often tell how powerful the video is just by seeing the pledges. The better the video, the bigger the money.

In July 2015, Adam Nimoy led Kickstarter's most successful campaign to date. The project was *For the Love of Spock*, a documentary film about Adam's father, Leonard Nimoy, aka *Star Trek*'s legendary Mr. Spock.[10] Adam's video tells a personal story about growing up under his famous dad's wing, and how much Mr. Spock meant to so many *Star Trek* fans across generations and around the world. The video is of high production quality, incorporating personal photos of Adam and his dad, and Adam explains why this campaign is so important. He connects with viewers as he explains what the film will offer them as *Star Trek* fans. He closes with the iconic Vulcan salute. It's a great example of how a well-prepared, thoughtful video brought in a tremendous ROI. The campaign far surpassed its $600,000 goal.

Outside of the crowdfunding model, marketing platforms like Vidyard can give you detailed analytics such as which segments of a video are getting the most play and where viewers are typically drop-ping, which can help you shape future content. This kind of data can help ROI by reducing future production costs and improving over-all viewer engagement.[11] If you are a college raising money through a video or selling a product, measuring the incoming money from the first time your video is distributed is another method of gauging ROI. Beyond the Internet, leaders interested in assessing the impact of their communications to stakeholders often rely on employee surveys and polls conducted by outside specialists.

We're early in the journey of measuring video's financial ROI, but it will become easier as the science and data evolve. Anecdotally, many of the best companies in the world make video a priority. CCO Tim Cook has taken over the reins from Steve Jobs as Apple's video communicator-in-chief. Richard Branson touts his entrepreneurial creds in a TED talk.[12] SAS CEO Jim Goodnight is in a number of vid-eos[13] that inform his employees about benefits and how much he gets out of chance meetings with everyday workers and learning what they are up to. These prominent leaders can't measure dollars in vs. dollars out on each film, but they still make video a part of their leadership journey. It's how their tribe has gotten to know who they are and what they stand for. That certainly counts for something.

Return on Investment—Key Ideas

▶ It's nearly impossible to measure the financial ROI of video when you're not using it to drive transactions.

▶ When measuring video's value, it helps to look at ROI through a different lens: Return on Inspiration and Return on Imagination. Think: How has your video inspired others to action? How has it helped them see your vision and embrace it?

▶ A great video's return on investment is often unpredictable. For some companies, strong videos have gone as far as inadvertently recruiting great new talent to their team.

▶ Today's most prominent leaders make video a priority. It's how they connect with their tribe worldwide, and it's the reason so many of us feel we know these leaders as humans.

Leveraging Video in Times of Crisis

B y now, I've made you well aware of the power of video. You can leverage it in just about any scenario, whether you're introducing yourself as a new leader, launching a product, recruiting new team members, or updating your tribe on the latest goings-on. Once you get comfortable in front of the lens, you'll probably want to use video more and more—and with good reason. It's an incredibly effective medium for connecting with your audience in an age when we rarely see all parties involved face-to-face.

This book's advice will prep you for any video, but I've dedicated this chapter to one of video's most challenging—and powerful—uses: crisis management. How leaders handle crisis and recovery can make leaders and their organizations stronger. We've talked about how video is the next best thing to in-person interactions, and this truth is especially important in times of crisis. People want to *hear and see* a leader telling them what's going on. Since you typically can't be in the same room with everyone affected by a crisis, video will help you personally connect with your audience when they need you the most. Video is also the fastest way to tell your story before the news media, or social media, put their own spin on it.

Crisis management is one of the toughest challenges for leaders. Often, they're so busy being in two places at once that they're caught off guard or even worse, not given all the facts they need to make timely decisions. Adding fuel to the fire is the media and its scary half-brother, social media. The hunger for any news, good or bad, is insatiable, and its viral momentum can accelerate a crisis event to speeds unheard of only a decade ago. If you've hired the right people to advise and help you, the odds are you will regain control. Often this means keeping your foot off the brake pedal and steering ever so lightly on the black ice.

Part of maneuvering your way over that black ice is being in careful communication with the people who expect to hear from you. You might cringe at the idea of getting on camera in the middle of a fiasco, but it's one of the most important things you need to do. Anything less may appear cowardly or make it look like you just don't care. Remember the world's response when George W. Bush was slow to react to the news of Hurricane Katrina? When disaster strikes, people demand to hear from their leader—quickly. And unfortunately, an email or any other easy way out just won't do. Unless you have the luxury of getting everyone involved in one room, you'd be wise to get in front of the camera as soon as you can.

I'm not saying this to alarm you. The truth is, if you're already investing in your on-camera performance for communicating in *good* times, you'll be in much better shape in moments of crisis, too. Everything you've learned in this book so far will help you—but keep reading for ideas to keep in mind when things gets especially hairy.

GETTING IT RIGHT ON CAMERA IN TIMES OF CRISIS

Apologies, sincere and heartfelt, can go a long way toward mitigating and laying a crisis to rest. What's key is to *keep being you* during the process. Depending on your message, you can be many versions of yourself: the-excited-about-your-vision you, the-empathetic-over-job-cuts you, the contrite you. Just never try to be someone you are not, especially on camera and even under the most extreme situations. Here are some additional guidelines.

Don't Panic

Your tribe will be looking to you to calm their fear. Communicate clearly that there is a way out of the problem, and give viewers a sense of hope. GM CEO Mary Barra offers a great example of keeping calm and spelling out next steps in a video addressing her company's new approach to safety evaluations and recalls. She says, "If we identify an issue that could possibly affect your safety, we are acting quickly. . . . We've conducted recalls involving fewer than one hundred vehicles, which demonstrates how quickly we're reacting when we become aware of an issue. . . . We're guided by one overriding goal: doing what's best for you, our customers."[1] At a time when her company's reputation was on the line, Barra made it clear why customers could still trust GM.

Be Direct

Tell viewers exactly what occurred, including the when, why, and where. Former Coty CEO Bernd Beetz always makes this a top priority in his videos. "I'm very direct. I never play politics," he says. "I always say things how they are at that point in time. I gain the confidence of people and make sure I always satisfy them and am in synch with their interests."[2]

Speak from the Heart

This is not the time to be polished and slick—in fact, there's never a time for that. Be yourself, be authentic. Visualize a proxy for your audience, a loved one or a good neighbor. How would you break the news? Be aware of your body posture. Stand tall; don't slump. Don't look like you are trying to hide.

Be Aware of Context

Authenticity is only part of the tool kit. It's also important to pay attention to your language and the context in which you're delivering your message. Yes, speak from the heart, but remember that there is a time and a place for everything. When BP CEO Tony Hayward apologized for the destruction his company's oil spill brought to the Gulf Coast in 2010, his message was sincere, but his timing was all wrong. He starts strong by saying, "I'm sorry for the massive disruption it's caused their lives," when speaking of the people affected by the spill. But he lost all credibility when he went on to say, "There's no one who wants this over more than I do. I'd like my life back."[3]

Those last five words spurred a PR nightmare for Hayward, with backlash even coming from White House press secretary Robert

Gibbs, who said of the eleven people who died on BP's oil rig, "There are eleven people that we'd all like to have their lives back."[4] It turns out, nobody felt sympathy for the inconvenienced CEO at a time when lives were being destroyed because of his company's mistake. Sincerity matters, but not if you're tone deaf to the larger issues at stake.

"Regrets are illuminations come too late."

—JOSEPH CAMPBELL

Go Where the Crisis Is

Step away from the corner office—your proverbial ivory tower—and get to the scene of the crisis if you can. You can't connect with your people if you treat this like a long-distance job. Rudy Giuliani knew this when he got on camera to respond to the 9/11 terror attacks on the World Trade Center. Elected mayor of New York City in 1994, his career was in tatters by 2001. But immediately following the attacks, he made all the right moves. Instead of seeking safer ground, he stayed in Manhattan, close to the epicenter of the attack. On camera (and in person) Giuliani urged calm while expressing empathy. On one occasion, he said, "My heart goes out to all the innocent victims of the horrible and vicious act of terrorism. And our focus now has to be to save as many lives as possible."[5] He didn't dress or act differently than before. He was still the mayor, but a much more serious and thoughtful version.

In the years that followed, the 9/11 Commission would blame the mayor for a general lack of preparedness that contributed to the chaos.

Nevertheless, immediately after the attack, he was careful with his manner, his words, and the locations where he held interviews and press conferences. By the end of his term, Giuliani had reinvented himself as an influential leader.

Bring in Others' Stories

Seeing people's responses to a crisis often ignites my hope for humanity. It's incredible to witness how difficult moments can bring out the best in people. Everyday people turn into heroes who do extraordinary things. To that end, sometimes the best way to show your camaraderie in a crisis is by not saying anything at all. Instead, highlight others' stories. Video can be your impetus to tell the heroic stories that unite us and help us understand our common journey. They make us more human.

We used exactly this approach when creating a post–Hurricane Katrina video for Medco (now Express Scripts). Our video captured the company in New Orleans as employees ran a portable pharmacy that distributed free medicine to anyone who needed it. Employees spoke directly to the camera about their experience helping others during such devastating times. While it was amazing to see the positive impact their work had in the community, equally touching was seeing how life changing the experience had been for the employees. One woman said, "It's been the highlight of my career to be down here helping people." These everyday workers turned into heroes as they left their families at home and slept in trailers so they could help people in need.

We also highlighted employee stories in a post–9/11 video for Nextel (now Sprint). No corporate message could rival hearing firsthand, from the people on the ground, how employees worked tirelessly to facilitate communication between lower Manhattan and the outside world. One employee recounted, "We rallied together to start gathering equipment because we knew communications were going to be needed." As they told their story, it was clear that each person made the personal choice to stay on the scene until they could connect Ground Zero relief workers with others who could help. These weren't your ordinary work anecdotes. They were stories of people who were deeply proud to sacrifice their comfort to serve others.

These videos were a reminder that life has more meaning when our actions have a purpose—and especially when that purpose is to help others. The stories also showed that it is an amazing feeling to work for a company that has a larger purpose, especially when you have the chance to serve people within that purpose.

Not every piece of advice here will apply to you in a moment of crisis. If you're feeling stressed about what to do, remember—again and again—that you're not in this alone. Work closely with your trusted advisors to craft a message that speaks to your audience's concerns. Remember that your audience doesn't want to hear about *you* unless you're talking about what you're doing to help *them*.

Let's take a closer look at how two other leaders took to video in a crisis.

Damage Control

Sometimes a crisis is self-inflicted. We all have those duh! moments, when we wish we'd taken a few extra moments to think before we said or did something. You might not be surprised to hear this by now, but you can turn to video to address those moments, too.

This is especially effective if your mistake happened on video in the first place. Should you make a mistake on camera, the road to recovering from it is going *back* on camera and making things right. You must acknowledge your error ASAP and carefully apologize to your audience with as much sincerity as you can muster. I cited Microsoft CEO Satya Nadella as an example of a great performance on camera, but he was by no means batting a thousand.

In spite of his brilliant corp comm team, Nadella managed to insult close to his entire audience in a video that covered his 2015 guest appearance at the Grace Hopper Celebration of Women in Computing conference. When it was brought to his attention that women make only seventy-eight cents to every dollar earned by men, Nadella's answer implied that rather than asking for a raise, women should have faith that they will somehow be rewarded over the long term. "That might be one of the [women's] additional superpowers, that quite frankly, women who don't ask for raises have," he said. "Because that's good karma. It will come back." Seized by media critics and many employees as a sexist remark, the video went viral and prompted Nadella to send an email to all Microsoft employees saying he answered the question "completely wrong."

Nadella also appeared in interviews on CNBC and *USA Today* where again he said his comments on women's pay were "completely wrong" and that his misstep has been "a very humbling and learning experience for me."

On camera he told *USA Today* that he now realized what "a raw nerve" his comments struck and how many women feel "the system has actually not worked for them."

Nadella then backed up his apology by adding that he checked for any evidence of a gender-based pay gap at Microsoft and found no disparity, that jobs with the same title and level had a "tight band" of 0.5 percent difference between them. Still, he added, more work needed to be done to make his industry more of a meritocracy.[6]

The CEO continued to take measures I'd call authentic actions. One of them took the form of a memo to staff saying the company was launching a diversity initiative to increase training in making the workplace more inclusive.

HOW ONE CEO *ALMOST* GOT IT RIGHT

In April of 2015, Blue Bell Creameries CEO Paul Kruse took to the camera after reports that his ice cream products were contaminated by *Listeria monocytogenes*. In a video posted on Vimeo and through an accompanying written release, Kruse swore that Blue Bell was "committed to doing the 100 percent right thing, and the best way to do that is to take all of our products off the market until we are confident that they are all safe." Kruse then went on to clearly outline all the steps his company was taking to protect his customers from any further outbreaks. He listed a phone number people could call and urged them to check the company website for up-to-date information. At the end of the on-camera message, he said, "We are heartbroken about this situation" and "committed to getting it right."[7]

This leader got it totally right—except for one thing. He either wasn't telling the truth or didn't know that as far back as 2013 his company knew about the bacteria contamination.[8] Either way, as the leader of the organization, he was responsible for its conduct.

The contrast between Nadella's and Kruse's actions highlights a critical point in crisis management: You must follow your message with real actions if you're going to accomplish anything. Of course, you should do this in good times and in bad, but it will never be more important than when you're trying to get your organization back on stable ground. If your message is not backed by immediate, authentic actions, you will only make your situation worse.

To be fair, you can't exactly compare a regional ice cream company to Microsoft, or the magnitude of each company's crisis. The food manufacturer struggled with a potentially fatal product contamination, while the global tech behemoth was dealing with a verbal slipup. But there's still a lot to learn here. A month after Blue Bell's listeria outbreak went public, it was announced that they were laying off 37 percent of their 3,900 employees and putting another 1,400 on partially paid furlough. They also announced they'd be reducing salaries for their remaining staff.[9] Of course, this all wasn't the result of their leader's video performance, but the lack of authenticity behind that performance may have played a role in the company's nosedive. Who knows what would have happened had Blue Bell and its leaders addressed the listeria contamination when it was discovered back in 2013? Perhaps they wouldn't have had to close operations for months and lose their people in the meantime.

Be honest. Own your mistakes. Act quickly. Be Authentic. Words of wisdom for any leader, at any time—but especially useful if you're addressing your tribe in times of crisis.

Leveraging Video in Times of Crisis—Key Ideas

▶ The way you handle a crisis and recovery can make both you and your organization stronger. Since you likely can't be in the same room with everyone affected by a crisis, leverage video to help you connect with your audience when they need you the most.

▶ Apologies, sincere and heartfelt, can go a long way toward mitigating and laying a crisis to rest. What's key is to *keep being you* during the process.

▶ Make sure to follow your video message with authentic actions if you hope to mitigate a crisis.

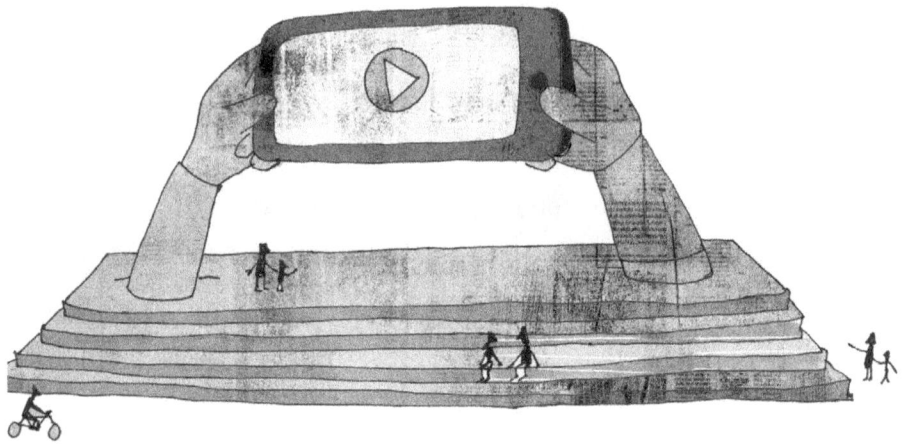

16

Creating Your Legacy

"The process of becoming a leader is similar,
if not identical, to becoming a fully integrated
human being."

—WARREN BENNIS

If you've read this book, you're now armed with the tools you'll need for more authentic, engaging video performances. Here's the boon: If you leverage video for all that it offers, your appearances can affect so much more than your company culture, or even your bottom line. They can change the world.

This may sound like a weighty promise, but think about how many people your company, your university, your nonprofit, or your political campaign touches. Yes, you have your employees, your customers, your strategic partners, but how about your local community and schools? Even if you're not literally working with these groups, your stakeholders are, and you have a profound opportunity to influence their everyday lives. This idea reminds me of an old saying:

> When I was a young man, I wanted to change the world. I found it was difficult to change the world, so I tried to change my nation. When I found I couldn't change the nation, I began to focus on my town. I couldn't change the town, so I tried to change my family. Now, as an old man, I realize the only thing I can change is myself, and suddenly I realize that if long ago I had changed myself, I could have made an impact on my family. My family and I could have made an impact on our town. Their impact could have changed the nation and I could indeed have changed the world.

People have credited this maxim to everyone from an AD 1100 monk to Rumi. Whoever said it, it's as true today as it was thousands of years ago. The best—and really, the only—way we can change the world is by starting with ourselves.

So what does this have to do with your video performance? Well, part of how we change ourselves is by telling our story and by connecting with others through our story. In today's business world, telling your story means appearing on video—and creating an environment where others can do the same.

I've mentioned a CEO who hated being on camera so much that he was thrilled at the idea of cutting the video budget so he wouldn't have to do it anymore. He was mostly joking (though not entirely!) and wise enough to keep the budget. If he had cut it, he wouldn't have just nixed a difficult task—he would have robbed his colleagues of the chance to tell their own story. It's up to top leadership to create an environment that encourages the company and its people to share their stories. Whether it's you on camera, or you're supporting the story being told by others, it all starts with you.

Your stories can help your community understand what your company stands for, its goals and aspirations, and how they fit within that journey. This is perhaps one of the biggest legacies you can leave. Because when you look back at the end of your career and see how many lives you've influenced, how many communities you've changed, how many jobs you've provided, or how many people you've educated, those people are going to tell the story of how they intersected with your organization even if they've never met you. These are the ripples in the pond that start with the true stories you tell from the heart.

I opened this book with a quote from street artist Banksy. It reads, "Film is incredibly democratic and accessible. It is probably the best option if you actually want to change the world." This point has been proven throughout history by leaders who took to video to drive social change, from Martin Luther King Jr. to Al Gore to Pope Francis. The opposite is also true. From tyrants like Hitler to terror groups like ISIS, propaganda films have been used to spread ideas, incite turmoil, and draw followers. That's because there is a demand in society for connection. Humans are pack animals, and we need to connect with others in order to thrive. If leaders can't make those connections with people in person, they have to do it on video.

In a way, video can help build a digital small town of sorts between you and your tribe when the real thing isn't possible. Perhaps you find it difficult to look one of your followers or customers in the eye at the local coffee shop or church function, but you can make a one-on-one connection with them through video. Today millennials are lucky enough to be able to click on any number of social media sites and see their leaders literally change society for the better. Icons like Ellen DeGeneres and author Dan Savage (through his *It Gets Better* video campaign) have helped millions of young people feel comfortable coming out in a society where gay marriage is now legal and a part of popular culture. By telling your story, you can influence society and where it's going. And it always starts with one person talking to another.

Now understand that there's a big difference between leaders who make great videos and those who change the world. Those who make a difference live their message every day. Lip service isn't enough. The world needs to see that you live your values all the time.

Early in my career, I worked at Pittsburgh's PBS station, WQED. At the time the host of a certain WQED TV show was known for being especially forgiving of his employees. Several members of his crew had struggled with substance abuse or had faced run-ins with the law. Despite this, their leader always gave them another chance. He held their jobs for them while they took time off to get their lives back in order. He offered help to anyone who needed it. While he was beloved for influencing the lives of his TV viewers, this leader was just as influential—if not more so—among the people with whom he worked every day.

You've probably heard of this guy—it was Fred Rogers, the host of *Mister Rogers' Neighborhood.*

Rogers was most known for the life lessons he imparted to his young viewers. They were the whole reason he started a career in television. He said in a CNN interview, "I went into television because I hated it so, and I thought there was some way of using this fabulous instrument to nurture those who would watch and listen."[1]

Over the years, he helped children deal with typical fears that prey on the hearts of the very young: fears of haircuts, the first day of school, how to deal with bullies; and the more deep and complicated issues of divorce, death, and war. I remember observing my little brother as he watched Mr. Rogers. It was the first time I'd noticed the power of speaking directly to the camera. Rogers talked to each child as if he were having a one-on-one conversation. He'd say things like, "Can you go get your coloring book?" and then wait a few seconds while the child fetched the item. It's a small detail, but this personal touch is part of how Rogers built trust with his viewers.

Rogers's kind and gentle manner made him a relatable person on-screen, but most people don't know how deeply he lived out those virtues in his everyday life.

Perhaps Rogers would have been as popular among children if he'd been a tyrannical boss behind the scenes. But I doubt he would have become such a beloved and iconic leader if he hadn't lived out his message of kindness and understanding when the cameras stopped rolling. By being as kind offscreen as he was on, he changed the lives of many employees who may not otherwise have had the opportunity to improve their situation.

I've said that a simple way to look at authenticity is to see it as writing your own story. Each time you appear on video, you're unveiling a new chapter. Well, it's one thing to tell a story and another thing entirely to embody that story. You are accountable for living up to the message you put out in the world.

The great thing is that if you do live the story you're writing, you're only going to want to make it better. You'll want to build a better you, and with that, a better company.

To those who have already put hours into improving their performances, it's my belief the advice in this book will get you to the next level. If you embrace the principles here with your whole heart, they can influence so much more than your video appearances. They may have a ripple effect through your whole organization and become the fabric of your legacy as a leader.

IT'S ABOUT SO MUCH MORE THAN VIDEO

Many of us grew up with the common belief that great leaders are decisive, clever, results-oriented, and sometimes heartless individuals. It seemed that all that counted to these driven people was the bottom line; all that mattered was winning. Indeed, many leaders out there still adhere to this model. I've met and filmed leaders who use fear and bullying "to get the job done." Certainly if you are a CEO, educational leader, or head of any company, you must never lose sight of productivity and the bottom line, but fewer leaders are getting away with doing this anymore at their people's expense.

The concept of leadership is evolving into a new model, and just in time. Paradoxically, breathtaking advances in digital technology are accelerating as tyrannical governments and fear-based business practices are collapsing. Social networking, cell phone videos, and other high-speed media are throwing a harsh light on the darker, narcissistic side of leadership. Instances of CEOs resigning for submitting false expense reports, government leaders covering up extramarital affairs with monetary payoffs, and chairmen of financial institutions committing massive fraud are being exposed every day. These are disquieting times, but they can also provide opportunities for trustworthy leaders to rise to the challenge. We can make a critical and positive difference in the world through a different kind of leadership, one not only steeped in authenticity but also channeled through heart.

At a time when traditional and social media are outing leaders' insufferable practices, true leaders can leverage video to show they are the kind of person others actually *want* to follow. The benefits of this approach can't be underestimated. On the most basic level, it will be good for business. People won't want to go to your school, work for you, invest in your company, or do anything else you might ask of them if they don't see you as someone they can trust and want to follow.

But the advantages run much deeper than your bottom line. By being your true self on camera, you become a living example of a leader who cares about how her organization affects the world. Open communication shows you care about your people, your work, and your mission. Why would anyone want to follow you if you didn't lead with such heart? Would *you* want to align yourself with someone who didn't seem to care about the people, the work, the bigger picture? Most people don't. They want to follow real leaders who care about the integrity of their work.

BUILDING YOUR LEGACY EVERY DAY

You build your legacy every time you go on camera. Historians interested in your leadership, your company, or your attitude toward things will be looking to these digital signposts. I was recently speaking with the head of HR at a major tech company, and she was remarking at how companies like Apple, Google, and Cisco were much better known than her company. I pointed out that they're better known because they're constantly telling their story, and because of that, people gradually came to learn what those companies stand for. This is true for any organization. Each time you connect with your tribe, they start to understand what kind of company they'll be doing business with, what kind of investment they've made, and whether or not they want to work with you.

Being true to yourself allows you to be real every time you go on camera. It creates an environment where people really can—and want to—follow you. The virtuous circle flows through your company and through every person your company touches. Imagine a world where people are transparent and true. I'm not talking about being soft or touchy-feely—just forthright and honest. If every business in the world were like that, wouldn't the world be a better place? Couldn't we change the world together? It all starts in that journey to authenticity that allows you to be the best you can be on camera.

I once studied with a wise, legendary acting teacher who told me, "Vern, you'll never have more in your art than you have in your life." As I've reflected on this idea over the years, I've realized this is as true in business as it is in art. The businesses you lead will never have more in them than you have in your life. Look at the most successful and beloved leaders, and those who were eventually found to be gaming the system. Those who showed who they are—on and offscreen—and lived those values through everyone they met, are the ones who truly went on to change the world.

Creating Your Legacy—Key Ideas

▶ Your videos have the potential to change the world if you leverage all that the medium has to offer.

▶ Telling your story and connecting with others through stories is the first step to changing the world through video.

▶ It doesn't matter how great your video presentations are if you don't live your message off camera.

▶ You build your legacy every time you go on camera as you reveal the kind of leader you are and draw a tribe of people who want to follow you.

Acknowledgments

I was telling my lunch companions about the book I was considering writing when I opened a fortune cookie that read, "You are a lover of words. Someday you will write a book." Some serendipitous moments are too perfect to be ignored!

To know me is to know that I am surrounded by books. Jeff Bezos may have added a wing to his house with my Amazon purchases alone.

I would love to say I "wrote" this book, but like many great creative endeavors, it was a collaboration. I am grateful to the many people who helped along the way.

Deepest thanks and acknowledgments go to the following people:

David N. Meyer, someone whose writing I love and whose passion for music, film, and books is unequaled. David taught me how to shape the series of insights and stories into the outline that grew into this book.

My longtime friend Steve Eder, whom I met in the basement of WQED toiling over TV specials. Steve is a true connoisseur of words and stories, and one of my favorite writers. Thanks for sharpening, focusing, and helping me connect these ideas.

Maria Gagliano, for editing, inspiring, keeping all the parts moving forward, and for reminding me to always keep the reader front and center. I thank my lucky stars that the universe connected me with you.

Taylor Lee, for the illustrations throughout the book that add style and meaning.

The interviewees and experts—Mark Block, Michael Chomet, Jordan LaMaire, and Chris Mushinskie for the editing process, Bret Curran for the teleprompter chapter, and fellow filmmakers James Tusty and Klaus Schiang-Franck on directing business executives.

The real heroes of this book and my highest inspiration—the business and institutional leaders who allowed me a peek behind the curtain of their businesses, colleges, and nonprofits to tell their stories. There is no greater honor than having their trust. Thank you to Michele Scannavini, Bernd Beetz, Vince Forlenza, Paul Bisaro, Georgia Nugent, and Daniel Weiss.

The thought leaders and practitioners in corporate communication, PR, and education, who craft stories—Mary Lou Ambrus, Bob Florance, Jon Pepper, Tina Orlando, Colleen White, Michael Goodman, Charlie Mayr, Jack Trout, Russell Amerasekera, and Tony Cicatiello.

The scientists and social researchers who continue to do breakthrough research that informed and inspired this book—Brené Brown, Amy Cuddy, Martin Seligman, Abraham Maslow, and Daniel Goleman.

The fantastic publishing team at Greenleaf—Justin Branch, Tyler

LeBleu, Carrie Jones, Sally Garland, Nathan True, and Kimberly Lance—who believed in this project from day one.

The book's researchers—Elizabeth H. Tilley, PhD, and Leah Borst.

My core group of trusted advisors, who have long been by my side on this journey of discovery and growth and without whom I could not be successful—Paul DelFino who taught me about leadership one story at a time; Siobhan Murphy, a brilliant and soulful coach who helped me understand if you want to change your business, you have to change yourself; and Julie Cucchi, the brand guru behind 98.6 and extractor of Tribe's DNA.

The people who read early drafts and asked insightful questions that enabled me to think more deeply about these truths—Staffan Ehde, Anthony Vagnoni, Chris Boebel, Dana Rubin, Elsie Maio, Blair Enns, Rebecca Carrier, Chiara Basso, Caitlin Teresa Finnegan, Khiara McMillin, David Lyman, Barbara Hennessy, and Scott McDowell.

The folks at Tribe Pictures, my second family, who live and breathe the power of film and stories every day, and who share the belief that if we can shape our clients' stories truthfully, we can impact the future for the better—Lu Borges, the book's project manager, who with a constant smile kept me on task and on point; Catherine Jarrett and Jason Carubia, my assistants, who helped me balance my passion for this project with the day-to-day time commitments of running a successful business; and all of you, too, for your continued support—Sharon Gernshcimer, Jessica Casale, Alexandra Beni, Cindy Murphy, Bonnie Steir, and Jon Huberth.

These excellent business teachers—Marshall Goldsmith, Richard Leider, David C. Baker, Josh Klenoff, and Harvard Business School's Linda Applegate, Royce Yudkoff, and Richard Ruback.

The International Quorum of Motion Pictures, who celebrate the transformative power of film and business across countries, genres, and topics. The open exchange of ideas among fellow production company owners has been an invaluable source of support and inspiration.

My teachers in the noble and empowering profession of drama— Gerald Patterson, Harlene Marley, Tom Turgeon, Jim Michaels, Michael Howard, Bob Prosky, Stella Adler, Bobby Lewis, Arthur Penn, Anthony Abeson, and Jack Garfein. My desire to pull off the mask and reveal what is beneath started with my love of drama.

And last, my parents, Bill and Mary Ann, for always encouraging me to pursue my passions; my children, Gibson and Grace, who inspire me every day; and my loving wife, Mary Jo, for her sacrifice, support, and encouragement as I continue my journey to authenticity.

Notes

Introduction

1. Michael Goodman, in conversation with the author, December 2014.

2. David Brancaccio, in conversation with the author, March 2016.

3. John C. Maxwell, *The 21 Irrefutable Laws of Leadership*, 10th Anniversary edition (Nashville: Thomas Nelson, Inc., 2007), 13.

Chapter 1

1. Kayla Webley, "How the Nixon-Kennedy Debate Changed the World," *TIME*, September 23, 2010, http://content.time.com/time/nation/article/0,8599,2021078,00.html.

2. N.R. Kleinfield, "New Style in Industry Film Making," *The New York Times*, March 31, 1982, http://www.nytimes.com/1982/03/31/business/new-style-in-industry-film-making.html.

3. Ibid.

4. Paul Vitello, "Leo-Arthur Kelmenson, Ad Man Who Helped to Save Chrysler, Dies at 84," *The New York Times*, September 3, 2011, http://www.nytimes.com/2011/09/04/business/leo-arthur-kelmenson-ad-executive-dies-at-84-helped-to-save-chrysler.html?ref=topics&_r=0.

5. "Cisco Visual Networking Index: Forecast and Methodology, 2015-2020," Cisco, June 1, 2016, http://www.cisco.com/c/en/us/solutions/collateral/service-provider/visual-networking-index-vni/complete-white-paper-c11-481360.html.

6. Bill Millar, "Video in the C-Suite," *Forbes Insights*, 2010, http://images.forbes.com/forbesinsights/StudyPDFs/Video_in_the_CSuite.pdf.

7.   Ketchum, "Ketchum Leadership Communication Monitor," May 2014, http://www.ketchum.com/leadership-communication-monitor-2014.

8.   Dave Kehr, "Arthur Penn, Director of 'Bonnie and Clyde,' Dies," *The New York Times*, September 29, 2010, http://www.nytimes.com/2010/09/30/movies/30penn.html.

Chapter 2

1.   Jim Tusty in conversation with the author, October 2015.

2.   Joshua Freedman, "The Neural Power of Leadership: Daniel Goleman on Social Intelligence," *Six Seconds*, February 27, 2007, http://www.6seconds.org/2007/02/27/the-neural-power-of-leadership-daniel-goleman-on-social-intelligence/.

3.   Karin Badt, "Mirror Neurons and Why We Love Cinema: A Conversation with Vittorio Gallese and Michele Guerra in Parma," *The Huffington Post*, May 10, 2013, http://www.huffingtonpost.com/karin-badt/mirror-neurons-and-why-we_b_3239534.html.

4.   Tony Cicatiello in conversation with the author, April 2015.

5.   Mark Logue and Peter Conradi, *The King's Speech* (London: Quercus Books, 2010). "King George VI Addresses the Nation," BBC, http://www.bbc.co.uk/archive/ww2outbreak/7918.shtml.

6.   Rob Goffee and Gareth Jones, "Managing Authenticity: The Paradox of Great Leadership," *Harvard Business Review*, December 2005, https://hbr.org/2005/12/managing-authenticity-the-paradox-of-great-leadership.

7.   Jonathan Martin and Amie Parnes, "McCain: Obama not an Arab, crowd boos," *Politico*, October 10, 2008, http://www.politico.com/news/stories/1008/14479.html.

8.   Elon Musk interviewed by Joseph Gordon-Levitt, "Elon Musk on SpaceX's long term goal – Mars (2014)," YouTube video, 3:08, posted by "Elon Musk videos," June 8, 2015, https://www.youtube.com/watch?v=AYdz9sqXQ28.

9.   Ibid.

Chapter 3

1. Brené Brown, *Daring Greatly: How the Courage to Be Vulnerable Transforms the Way We Live, Love, Parent, and Lead* (New York: Avery, 2012).

2. Brené Brown, "The Power of Vulnerability," filmed June 2010, TEDxHouston video, 20:19, https://www.ted.com/talks/brene_brown_on_vulnerability?language=en.

3. David Seidler, *The King's Speech* (screenplay), See-Saw Films/Bedlam Productions, http://www.pages.drexel.edu/~ina22/splaylib/Screenplay-Kings_Speech_The.pdf.

4. Tina Orlando in conversation with the author, December 2014.

5. Andre Agassi, *Open* (New York: Knopf, 2009), 187.

Chapter 4

1. Jim Tusty in conversation with the author, October 2015.

2. Vince Forlenza in conversation with the author, December 2014.

3. Klaus Schiang-Franck in conversation with the author, January 2016.

4. Bob Florance in conversation with the author, July 2015.

Chapter 5

1. Hans Christian Andersen, "The Emperor's New Clothes," *The Hans Christian Andersen Centre*, http://www.andersen.sdu.dk/vaerk/hersholt/TheEmperorsNewClothes_e.html.

2. Charlie Mayr in conversation with the author, December 2014 and January 2015.

3. Jon Pepper in conversation with the author, December 2014.

4. Ibid.

5. "The Executives' Disease?" The Boylston Group, http://www.theboylstongroup.com/e_disease.htm.

6. Jon Pepper in conversation with the author, December 2014.

7.   Tina Orlando in conversation with the author, December 2014.

8.   Russell Amerasekera in conversation with the author, February 2015.

Chapter 6

1.   Mark Bowden, "The Importance of Being Inauthentic," filmed September 2013, TEDxToronto video, 20:50, http://tedxtalks.ted.com/video/The-Importance-Of-Being-Inauthe.

2.   Jonathan Kalb, "Give Me a Smile," *The New Yorker*, January 12, 2015, http://www.newyorker.com/magazine/2015/01/12/give-smile.

3.   Martin E. P. Seligman, *Authentic Happiness* (New York: Free Press, 2002), 5.

4.   Richard Branson interviewed by *Time* magazine, "10 Questions for Richard Branson," *TIME* magazine video, 6:38, http://content.time.com/time/video/player/0,32068,1347878415_1721845,00.html.

5.   Jonathan Kalb, "Give Me a Smile," *The New Yorker*, January 12, 2015, http://www.newyorker.com/magazine/2015/01/12/give-smile.

6.   David A. Leopold and Gillian Rhodes, "A Comparative View of Face Perception," *Journal of Comparative Psychology* 124, no. 3 (August 2010), 233–251, http://www.ncbi.nlm.nih.gov/pmc/articles/PMC2998394/.

7.   Paul Ekman, "Micro Expressions," *Paul Ekman Group*, http://www.paulekman.com/micro-expressions/.

8.   Dacher Keltner and Paul Ekman, "The Science of 'Inside Out'," *The New York Times*, July 3, 2015, http://www.nytimes.com/2015/07/05/opinion/sunday/the-science-of-inside-out.html?_r=0.

9.   Mark Bowden, "The Importance of Being Inauthentic," filmed September 2013, TEDxToronto video, 20:50, http://tedxtalks.ted.com/video/The-Importance-Of-Being-Inauthe.

10. Jon Pepper in conversation with the author, December 2014.

11. Amy Cuddy, "Your Body Language Shapes Who You Are," filmed June 2012, TEDGlobal 2012, 21:02, https://www.ted.com/talks/amy_cuddy_your_body_language_shapes_who_you_are?language=en.

12. Ibid.

13. Bob Florance in conversation with the author, July 2015.

Chapter 7

1. Michael Caine, *Acting in Film* (New York: Applause Theatre & Cinema Books, 2000), 3.

2. Bill George in conversation with the author, April 2016

Chapter 8

1. Michele Scannavini in conversation with the author, October 2014.

2. Fred Kaplan, "The Evasions of Robert McNamara," *Slate*, http://www.slate.com/articles/arts/culturebox/2003/12/the_evasions_of_robert_mcnamara.html.

3. "Business Tips from Sara Blakely, Founder of Spanx by OPEN Forum," YouTube video, 3:09, posted by "American Express," March 19, 2012, https://www.youtube.com/watch?v=LFNcmlv7sQo.

4. Paul Bisaro in conversation with the author, January 2015.

5. Tina Orlando in conversation with the author, December 2014.

Chapter 9

1. Satya Nadella interviewed by Steve Clayton, "Satya Nadella: His first interview as CEO of Microsoft," YouTube video, 4:44, posted by "Microsoft," February 4, 2014, https://www.youtube.com/watch?v=T8JwNZBJ_wI.

2. David Zeiler, "Microsoft Stock Today: Five Ways Satya Nadella Woke a Laggard," *Money Morning*, February 4, 2015, moneymorning.com/2015/02/04/microsoft-stock-today-five-ways-satya-nadella-woke-up-a-laggard/.

Chapter 10

1. Tom Ackerman, Shauna Robertson, David O. Russell, Judd Apatow, Will Ferrell, Adam McKay, Christina Applegate et al., *Anchorman: The Legend of Ron Burgundy* (Glendale, CA: DreamWorks Home Entertainment, 2004).

2. "J.K. Simmons winning Best Supporting Actor," YouTube video, 3:03, posted by "Oscars," March 9, 2015, https://www.youtube.com/watch?v=EBoMKkmJEMg.

3. "etalk at the Oscars: J.K. Simmons," *etalk* video, 1:07, February 28, 2016, http://www.etalk.ca/?videoid=817400.

4. Tina Orlando in conversation with the author, December 2014.

5. Jon Pepper in conversation with the author, December 2014.

6. Paul Bisaro in conversation with the author, January 2015.

Chapter 11

1. http://filmmakeriq.com/.

2. Michele Scannavini in conversation with the author, October 2014.

3. "Susan Wojcicki: It's Never Too Late to Learn," YouTube video, 1:05, posted by "Code.org," November 17, 2014, https://www.youtube.com/watch?v=foywg7zXS9c.

Chapter 12

1. Bernd Beetz in conversation with the author, November 2014.

2. Vince Forlenza in conversation with the author, December 2014.

3. Paul Bisaro in conversation with the author, January 2015.

4. Ibid.

5. Bill Rosenthal, "The Only Way To Prepare To Give A Presentation," *Forbes*, June 19, 2013, http://www.forbes.com/sites/forbesleadershipforum/2013/06/19/the-only-way-to-prepare-to-give-a-presentation/.

6. Mike Evangelist, "Behind the Magic Curtain," *The Guardian*, January 5, 2006, http://www.theguardian.com/technology/2006/jan/05/newmedia.media1.

7. Neil deGrasse Tyson interviewed by Dave Davies, *Fresh Air*, NPR, February 27, 2014, http://www.npr.org/programs/fresh-air/2014/02/27/283496068/fresh-air-for-february-27-2014. Neil deGrasse Tyson, interviewed by Jon Stewart, *The Daily Show*, February 27, 2012, http://www.cc.com/video-clips/co5kzq/the-daily-show-with-jon-stewart-neil-degrasse-tyson.

Chapter 13

1. Kevin Spacey, "Kevin Spacey Teaches Acting," MasterClass video, 1:42, 2016, https://www.masterclass.com/classes/kevin-spacey-teaches-acting.

2. Constantin Stanislavski, *An Actor Prepares* (New York: Routledge, 1948).

3. "Makers Profile: Indra Nooyi," Makers.com video, 4:28, 2016, http://www.makers.com/indra-nooyi.

4. Elizabeth Blankespoor, Greg Miller, Brad Hendricks, "Perceptions and Price: Evidence from CEO Presentations at IPO Roadshows," Working Paper No. 3253, 2015, https://www.gsb.stanford.edu/faculty-research/working-papers/perceptions-price-evidence-ceo-presentations-ipo-roadshows.

5. Lee Simmon, "Elizabeth Blankespoor: In IPO Road Shows, the Messenger Is the Message," *Insights by Stanford Business*, July 21, 2015, https://www.gsb.stanford.edu/insights/elizabeth-blankespoor-ipo-road-shows-messenger-message.

6. Constantin Stanislavski, *An Actor Prepares* (New York: Routledge, 1948).

7. Daniel Weiss in conversation with the author, April 2015.

8. Ibid.

9. Ibid.

10. Ibid.

11. Ibid.

12. Elisha Goldstein, PhD, interviewed by Annie Daly, "What's *Actually* the Difference Between Mindfulness and Meditation?" *Women's Health*, September 12, 2014, http://www.womenshealthmag.com/life/mindfulness-vs-meditation.

13. Ibid.

14. Y. Tang, Q. Lu, X. Geng, E.A. Stein, Y. Yang, & M.L. Posner, "Short-term Meditation Induces White Matter Changes in the Anterior Cingulate," *Proceedings of the National Academy of Sciences* 107, no. 35 (August 31, 2010), 15649–15652, doi:10.1073/pnas.1011043107.

15. David Hamilton, "Visualizing the Perfect Performance," David R. Hamilton PhD (blog), September 12, 2012, http://drdavidhamilton.com/visualizing-the-perfect-performance/.

16. Amy Cuddy, "Your Body Language Shapes Who You Are," filmed June 2012, TEDGlobal 2012, 21:02, https://www.ted.com/talks/amy_cuddy_your_body_language_shapes_who_you_are?language=en. Amy Cuddy, *Presence* (New York: Little, Brown, 2015).

17. Dana R. Carney, Amy J. C. Cuddy, Andy J. Yap, "Power Posing – Brief Nonverbal Displays Affect Neuroendocrine Levels and Risk Tolerance," *Journal of the Association for Psychological Science* 21, no. 10 (October 2010), 1363–1368, doi:10.1177/0956797610383437. PMID 20855902.

18. Arthur W. Page Society, "Jack Welch on the Vital Role of the CCO," Arthur W. Page Society Page Turner (blog), April 13, 2015, http://www.awpagesociety.com/blog/jack-welch-on-the-vital-role-of-the-cco.

19. Paul Bisaro in conversation with the author, January 2015.

20. Brandel Chamblee, "Is Swing Coach Como the Right Fit for Woods?" *Golf Channel*, December 1, 2014, http://www.golfchannel.com/news/brandel-chamblee/como-right-fit-woods/.

21. "Checked Growth: How Burberry's Angela Ahrendts Is Steering the Company through a Volatile Economy," *Knowledge @ Wharton* (blog), November 20, 2008, http://knowledge.wharton.upenn.edu/article/checked-growth-how-burberrys-angela-ahrendts-is-steering-the-company-through-a-volatile-economy/.

22. Marshall Goldsmith, *What Got You Here Won't Get You There* (New York: Hachette, 2007), 154.

Chapter 14

1. Dave Kehr, "Arthur Penn, Director of 'Bonnie and Clyde,' Dies," *The New York Times*, September 29, 2010, http://www.nytimes.com/2010/09/30/movies/30penn.html.

2. Jack Welch and Suzy Welch, *The Real-Life MBA* (New York: HarperBusiness, 2015), 17.

3. Best Practices, LLC, "Corporate Communications Budget & Staffing Benchmarks: Are You Spending Too Much?," *PR Newswire*, June 22, 2006, http://www.prnewswire.com/news-releases/corporate-communications-budget--staffing-benchmarks-are-you-spending-too-much-56223792.html.

4. Towers Watson, "Clear Direction in a Complex World," 2011, https://www.towerswatson.com/en-CA/Insights/IC-Types/Survey-Research-Results/2012/01/2011-2012-Change-and-Communication-ROI-Study-Report.

5. "Using Employee Communication as a Business Process to Improve Financial Results," YouTube video, 1:03:41, posted by "ISM University," July 19, 2014, https://www.youtube.com/watch?v=j1aQhbJ2XlQ.

6. Adam Bryant, *The Corner Office* (New York: Times Books, 2011), 176.

7. "Container Store CEO Kip Tindell: Great Workers Deserve Great Salaries," *Big Think* video, 5:10, http://bigthink.com/videos/kip-tindell-pay-your-employees-well.

8. Molly Borchers, "Measuring the ROI of Public Relations: Five Experts Weigh In," *The Huffington Post*, March 26, 2014, http://www.huffingtonpost.com/molly-borchers/measuring-the-roi-of-publ_b_5021600.html.

9. Neil Davidson, "Your Kickstarter Is 85% More Likely to Succeed with a Video," *MWP Digital Media*, July 30, 2013, http://mwpdigitalmedia.com/blog/without-a-video-your-kickstarter-project-will-probably-fail/.

10. Adam Nimoy, "For the Love of Spock," Kickstarter video, 2:53, https://www.kickstarter.com/projects/adamnimoy/for-the-love-of-spock-a-documentary-film/description.

11. Vidyard, "Video: The New ROI Star of Marketing" (whitepaper), https://www.vidyard.com/video-roi-whitepaper/.

12. Richard Branson, "Life at 30,000 Feet," filmed March 2007, TED2007 video, 29:51, https://www.ted.com/talks/richard_branson_s_life_at_30_000_feet?language=en.

13. "SAS CEO Jim Goodnight on SAS' Great Employee Benefits," YouTube video, 4:15, posted by "SAS Software," October 25, 2012, https://www.youtube.com/watch?v=T5O3L6UdIGw.

Chapter 15

1. Mary Barra, "GM CEO Mary Barra Puts Recalls into Context," YouTube video, 1:40, posted by "General Motors," July 28, 2014, https://www.youtube.com/watch?v=4SS5Fn2vadk.

2.   Bernd Beetz in conversation with the author, November 2014.

3.   "BP CEO Tony Hayward: 'I'd Like My Life Back'," YouTube video, 0:35, posted by "climatebrad," May 31, 2010, https://www.youtube.com/watch?v=MTdKa9eWNFw.

4.   Jake Tapper, "BP Turns to Political Shop for $50 Million Ad Buy to Convince You the Company 'Will Get This Done' and 'Make It Right'," *ABC News* (blog), June 4, 2010, http://blogs.abcnews.com/politicalpunch/2010/06/bp-turns-to-political-shop-for-50-million-ad-buy-to-convince-you-the-company-will-get-this-done-and-.html.

5.   Michael Powell, "In 9/11 Chaos, Giuliani Forged a Lasting Image," *The New York Times*, September 21, 2007, http://www.nytimes.com/2007/09/21/us/politics/21giuliani.html.

6.   Ben Fox Rubin, "Microsoft CEO Takes Lessons from Gaffe about Women's Pay," CNET, October 20, 2014, http://www.cnet.com/news/microsoft-ceo-takes-lessons-from-gaffe-about-womens-pay/.

7.   "Statement from Blue Bell CEO and President Paul Kruse," Blue Bell video, 0:37, April 20, 2015, http://cdn.bluebell.com/ceo-video-message.

8.   Rachel Abrams, "Blue Bell Knew About Listeria Issues, F.D.A. Says," *The New York Times*, May 7, 2015, http://www.nytimes.com/2015/05/08/business/blue-bell-knew-about-listeria-issues-fda-says.html.

9.   Jesse Newman and David Kesmodel, "Blue Bell Will Lay Off 1,450 Employees," *The Wall Street Journal*, May 15, 2015, http://www.wsj.com/articles/blue-bell-will-lay-off-1-450-employees-1431721160.

Chapter 16

1.   "Pioneers of Television: Fred Rogers," PBS, http://www.pbs.org/wnet/pioneers-of-television/pioneering-people/fred-rogers/.

Index

About the Author

Veteran filmmaker, teacher, speaker, and industry thought leader Vern Oakley is CEO and creative director of Tribe Pictures, which he founded in 1986.

Vern has created films for *Fortune* 500 companies, nonprofit organizations, universities, and their leaders. His mission is to help humanize the world's most successful leaders and institutions, helping them to craft their stories and connect to the people who matter most. Personally, Vern has been on a lifelong journey to explore and express his own authenticity and to create meaningful human connections. To this end, he has studied with a variety of experts and institutions from Arthur Penn and the Actor's Studio to Harvard Business School.

A client of Vern's once bestowed on him the unofficial title "Business Artist." He believes this captures his comfort with both left- and right-brain endeavors and his passion for sharing these lessons with others.

www.ingramcontent.com/pod-product-compliance
Lightning Source LLC
Chambersburg PA
CBHW031845200326
41597CB00012B/277